Cartel City

By
Durell Eubanks

Cadmus Publishing
www.cadmuspublishing.com

Copyright © 2022 Durell Eubanks

Published by Cadmus Publishing
www.cadmuspublishing.com
Port Angeles, WA

ISBN: 978-1-63751-214-2
Library of Congress Control Number: 2022910565

All rights reserved. Copyright under Berne Copyright Convention, Universal Copyright Convention, and Pan-American Copyright Convention. No part of this book may be reproduced, stored in a retrieval system, or transmitted in any form, or by any means, electronic, mechanical, photocopying, recording or otherwise, without prior permission of the author.

This is a work of fiction; therefore, names, characters, places, and incidents are the products of the author's imagination or are used fictitiously. Any resemblance to actual events, locales, or persons, living or dead, is entirely coincidental.

Dedication

This book is lovingly dedicated to the strongest woman I know, my mother Louise Eubanks, who has always been by my side, whom has always given me words of encouragement. Even in my darkest times, she was there as my guiding light pushing me forward to achieve my goals. Every time I fell down and life became hard for me, she would say, get up, stand on your feet, you are not defeated. I believe in you. Mama, I just want to say thank you. The whole family loves you, your strength inspires us all. I can't wait to get back home so you can make me your homemade sweet potato pie that you know I love so much. Love you mother.

Acknowledgements

First I would like to thank God for allowing me to find myself in a place where many people are lost. I would like to thank my wife, Felicia, for always having my back and putting up with bullshit and sticking by my side through the ups and downs. You are greatly appreciated. To my brother Ricardo Banks salute bruh. To my daughters Areeon and Zynah for making me boss up. Everything Daddy does is for ya'll. To my Granny Motaver, Grandma Macy, My Uncle James, My Aunt Betty, Aunt Shirley, Aunt Sonya, Aunt Phyllis, Uncle Albert, Uncle Shawn. My whole family, I love ya'll. To everybody that supports me, Smoke, Tru, Debo, Lott, Tiny Wench, A.D, Shi, Big Pinn, seven big glit, Montana, Mattie Rich, Abdul Latif, 6/9, Ali, Shawn, T.Mack, Sp, T.Bone, KK, Fatima, Amira, Naomi, Raha, Rasheed, Aqueelah, Imam Yahya Shabazz, writers Katrina Hamilton and Amatullah, your articles in the Muslim Journal are beyond motivational, writer Hameem Habeeb. To my father, Henry Eubanks, I love you pops and I miss you. You will never be forgotten. Thank you for believing in me. I wish you could see everything I'm doing now. I know you would be proud.

Contents

Prologue 1
Chapter 1: The Beginning 4
Chapter 2: Money Time 15
Chapter 3: The Next Day 25
Chapter 4: Committed 35
Chapter 5: Gifts 45
Chapter 6: Hammer Time 56
Chapter 7: Hell is Hot 63
Chapter 8: Hood Magic 73
Chapter 9: What's Yours is Mine 80
Chapter 10: Where Ya At 100
Chapter 11: Dead Men Don't Talk 110
Chapter 12: Vengeance is Mine 118
Chapter 13: Goons Don't Play 126
Chapter 14: Warning Signs and Roots 134
Chapter 15: Married to the Family 143
Chapter 16: Devil's Motivation 152
Chapter 17: The Set Up 160
Chapter 18: Life of the Party 170
Chapter 19: Devils Die Too 177
Chapter 20: King of Spades 186
Chapter 21: Grim Reapers Calling 199
Chapter 22: Pain 209
Chapter 23: Invincible 229
Epilogue 247

Prologue

The couple sat on the couch hugged in each other's arms, as they watched an old re-run of The Wire. Rio had been working hard for his cousin Kanden making sure that the blocks ran smooth. It was his job to keep everything in order, and he did it well. Kanden had trusted Rio to run things because he had gotten sick and couldn't keep up with everything himself. The money was good, but there were plenty haters on the frontline as always. His new position with Kanden gave Rio power, power that a lot of other hustlers wanted. Kanden's rival Money-B had been moving in on Kanden territory with the intentions of pushing Kanden and his crew completely out. Bodies dropped on the regular as Kanden and Money-B's camp fought back and forth. Rio maintained the balance by having Money-B's top two hustlers murdered. Rio's new position had taken a lot of time from his marriage. Tonight was his downtime, his time to spend with his wife.

Outside Danger sat in his car with his two loaded .357's, tonight Rio had to go, Money-B had made that clear. When he paid Danger to execute the hit, he wanted it loud and ugly. A statement to be made, to put Kanden in his place. Danger sat in his old Nova smoking a blunt as he watched Rio's house. He had been staked out outside for hours. When he looked up at the house once more, he saw that the lights were now cut off. It was time to move. Danger checked his .357's making sure everything was in working order before he opened the door and exited his Nova.

Danger crept up to Rio's house silently. When he got to the front door he pulled his ski-mask over his skull, then he pulled a metal pin from his pocket, and began to pick the lock. Danger was not only a hitman he was a master safe cracker. It took him less than sixty seconds to pop the lock on Rio's front door. Once the door was opened Danger crept inside in a low crouch with his .357 held high gripped with both hands. As he traveled deeper inside Rio's house he could hear the sound of a woman moaning in pleasure. Danger followed the sound until he reached Rio's master bedroom stepping lightly sure of himself that he wouldn't make a sound to give away his position. Inside the bedroom he stood in the shadows as he watched Rio fuck his wife from behind. When he grew tired of the brief entertainment Danger raised his .357 and shot Rio in the back of the head, fragments of his skull and blood splattered as Rio fell forward from the pressure of the bullet that had just entered his skull. Terrified his wife began to scream. Danger walked closer to her gripping the smoking revolver in his hand with his right finger on his lips, an indication for her to be quiet. To Danger's surprise the sexy petite young woman lunged at him from the bed swatting at his face in a catlike motion. Danger lightly pushed her to the ground.

He watched as she fell to the floor. A grin appeared on his face a sinister smile of satisfaction.

"I was gonna let you live." Danger spat.

"Fuck you mother fucker. You killed my husband." Rio's wife spat in frustration as she stood up and sprinted toward Danger.

"So be it," Danger whispered raising his .357, he shot her in the face and watched as her lifeless body hit the floor. On his way out he bent down, and closed her eyes. Satisfied that his mission was complete Danger stood up and exited Rio's house. He sprinted to his Nova, jumped inside and pulled off. When Danger got safely home only then did he call Money-B on his burnout phone.

'Ring', 'Ring'.

"Hello." Money- B answered.

"It's done."

"Okay good." Was all Money-B said before hanging up the phone.

Chapter 1

The Beginning

Justice Santiago and his partner Amir Jackson pulled up to the Citco gas station bumping that new Kevin Gates. Justice parked and pulled out his phone to call one of his street Lieutenants to let him know he was at the spot.

After he hung up he reached into the ash-tray and pulled out a half a blunt and lit it up. 20 minutes went by before his Lieutenant Crazy K pulled up in his all black four runner. Crazy K parked beside Justice, and got out and hopped in the backseat of Justice's Caddy.

"Yo what's up Bro?"

"Not too much, you got that for me."

"Of course big bruh don't I always come thru?" Crazy K replied tossing a brown paper bag in Justice's lap.

Justice caught the bag and opened it to check the contents inside. After he was satisfied he reached over and hit the button to pop the trunk.

"Grab the book bag everything is inside. I'll meet you here sometime next week."

"I got cha Big Bro." Crazy K answered as he got out the backseat and grabbed the book bag out of the trunk slapping the trunk as he shut it back. Justice and Amir pulled off, with Crazy K heading in the opposite direction. Right before Justice got on the interstate he sped past a sitting state trooper.

"Shit," Justice cussed under his breath as he checked his rearview mirror seeing the trooper pull out hitting his blue lights. Justice hit the gas pushing his Cadillac CTS to the max. He shot past the intersection making a left turn, then a right turn trying his best to lose the committed Trooper as he headed down Old Country Road. Thinking fast he handed his nine to Amir.

"Yo when I bust this next right toss all the guns out the window." Justice spat his adrenaline shooting through the roof.

"Aite Bruh hit the gas on this bitch." Amir hollered while looking back and forth watching for the perfect time to toss the hammers. Justice busted a right then another right. Seeing the opportunity Amir tossed their hammers out the window being sure to watch where they landed so he could come back and pick them up. Justice still didn't slow down. He kept pushing his 2018 Cadillac to the max until he seen the road began to intersect. He made a quick left turn, just as the trooper rammed the side of his car causing his vehicle to flip through an old field knocking him unconscious. When he woke up he was in the hospital handcuffed to the bed with two officers sitting beside him.

"Yo what happened, what am I doing here?" Justice asked the pretty nurse as she walked over to him.

"You were in a car accident. You suffered a concussion, and a dislocated shoulder. You were very lucky, you've been out of it for two days." The nurse replied.

"What about the guy that was with me?"

"Amir Jackson he's fine he walked away without a scratch. The police have him in custody." The nurse informed nodding her head toward the two officers sitting beside him.

"Well this is all for now Mr. Santiago. I have other patients to attend to. He's all yours officers." The nurse said cutting her eye back at Justice before she walked out the door.

One of the officers stood up and read Justice his rights, then they let him know what he was being charged with. Justice smiled to himself knowing that they didn't find the hammers that Amir had thrown out the window. All of his charges were traffic charges. *He would be out in no time,* he thought to himself. Later that same day Justice was released from the hospital, and taken to the county jail where he was given a $250,000 bond.

Justice Santiago was a known street General, and everybody respected his gun game and his ability to control situations, and the fact that his late mother was a Queen pin. From birth his mother had taught him the game, everything came easy for him. He was a natural born hustler. He possessed the same skill as his mother, a professional at getting money and making things happen, also making people disappear if need be. When he walked in his cellblock with his arm in a sling everybody knew who he was. Shit the city belonged to him. The real question was who didn't know him. It was clear that the Alpha had just stepped in the Block.

"Stunna Boy," someone hollered from the top tier as they watched Justice come in.

"You better know it," Justice hollered back as he sat his mat and bedroll on the floor.

"Yo Gee clean that cell up and move your shit out so the Bro can get that cell," Tone hollered.

"I ain't trying to give my cell up." Gee replied in frustration.

"You can move out or we coming down there and we're throwing you out. It's your choice makes no matter to me. I need some Rec anyway," Tone spat.

"Come on Tone, I don't want no problems," Gee begged.

"Then move your shit before it's gets ugly for you partner," Tone spat.

30 minutes later Gee's cell was cleaned and all his property was thrown on the dayroom floor while Justice was having a conversation with someone he knew. Tone had sent someone downstairs to get Justice's stuff and put it in his cell for him.

"Yo where the fuck is my shit?" Justice hollered when he got off the phone.

"Cell 32 Big Bruh," Tone hollered.

Justice looked up and could have sworn he'd seen a ghost.

"Tone, damn fool. I haven't seen you in forever. Come down here and holler at me." Justice said walking into his cell, Tone walked in behind him, they shared a brief embrace.

"What you in for?" Tone asked.

"Traffic charges, reckless driving, speeding to elude, driving without a license, failure to stop at a red light. Shit crazy, but I'm good tho Amir threw the hammers out the window. I'm about to get on the phone, and call my girl Lisa, and tell her to come post my bond so I can get out of here."

"What you here for?" Justice asked.

"Shit bro I caught a body. Came home from work and found my girl in bed with another man. I snapped and deaded his ass."

"Damn, I'm sorry to hear that."

"I'm good with it. I should've killed my girl to, but I loved her too much. Fuck it. I don't regret it."

"Damn I don't know what to say, but thanks for the cell, you didn't have to do that."

"You good you are a Chapel Hill Stunna Boy like me, ain't noway you sleeping in the dayroom. Gee's a bitch ass nigga anyway he in here on a rape charge."

"Oh! That what it do Bro. Look let me hop on this phone real quick so I can call my girl."

"No problem bruh do your thing. I'll be upstairs if you need me." Tone replied then dapped Justice up, then he walked back upstairs. Justice walked over to the phone and dialed his girl's number.

'Ring', 'Ring'.

"Hello," Lisa answered.

"You have a collect call from 'Justice' from the Orange County Jail to accept this call please press five."

Lisa pressed five after hearing her boyfriend's name to accept the call.

"Hey baby." Justice said putting on his sexy voice.

"Hey Love, what happened?"

"I got caught up. I need you to come get me and Amir."

"Amir's locked up to?"

"Yeah I don't know what he's charged with. It couldn't be much since we didn't caught with anything."

"How much is your bond?"

"$250,000 thou."

"Damn boy, what did you do?"

"Caught a bunch of traffic charges, you coming or what?"

"You know I'm coming. Let me put some clothes on and call the Bondsman, then I'm on my way."

"Okay, I'll see you when you get here, love you."

"Love you too Baby."

When Justice got off the phone he went back to his cell and took a nap before he went and got himself in some more trouble that he didn't need right now. When he woke up he grabbed his towel, wash cloth, and soap and headed to the shower. When he finished he dried off and headed back to his cell to his surprise, he noticed Big Bruno standing by the doorway of his cell. Justice knew what it was but he didn't pay it any mind. Crazy K had already told him what happened.

"Bruno Cortez why am I not surprised?"

"Justice, you know we gotta shoot it. Ya boy Crazy K jumped my brother down in the Bottoms." Bruno spat. "I don't care about your shoulder, so don't even think of ducking no rec."

"Ducking rec you got me fucked up. Let me get dressed." Justice spat clearly frustrated with Bruno's bullshit.

"Yeah you do that. I'll be upstairs waiting." Bruno replied then he walked off.

Justice went in his cell and put his shoes on then took off upstairs. On the way up he ran into Tone.

"Yo Bruh what's up? Why you moving so fast." Tone asked.

"That clown Bruno pulled up on me and said he wanted to go a couple rounds. I'm bout to go up here and feed his ass real quick."

"You talking about Bruno from the Bottoms?"

"Yeah that's him."

"What! Ain't noway, come on Bruh." Tone said as they both took off headed towards Bruno's cell.

"Yo you got a problem with my people?" Tone spat.

"Yeah he already know what it is, you don't have anything to do with this." Bruno said.

"Hell if I don't! He a Stunna Boy." Tone spat as he ran in Bruno's cell punching him in the face, hitting him with a mean combination. Justice without a second thought instantly fell in line, hitting Big Bruno over the head with the lock he had stashed in his pants before he left his cell. Hearing the loud commotion a couple of Tone's friends ran in Bruno's cell and began to beat Bruno senseless. Unconscious they drug Bruno out of his cell and threw him downstairs where more Stunna Boys continued to kick and stomp on his head until the Jailer came rushing in spraying mace and shooting inmates with stun guns. Through all the chaos Justice kept beating Bruno until he was hit with a taser, knocking all the fight out of him as he fell to the ground shaking foaming from the mouth as the Jailer turned up the heat.

After order was restored Justice, Tone, and a few of his homeboys were dragged out the block and thrown in the hole. Bruno was taken to the infirmary in critical condition. The very next day the Jailer that had stunned Justice appeared at his cell door banging on his cell window.

"Get your bitch ass up." The Jailer shouted.

Still badly bruised from the beating he had taken at the hands of the jailers Justice got up from his bed and slowly walked to his door.

"Oh you think you're tough. Coming in my jail thinking you running shit, this ain't the streets."

"Fuck you Pig." Justice spat through swollen lips as he stared the jailer in the eye, then he spit on the glass.

"We'll see how much shit you talk in a few minutes." The Jailer replied. Then two more jailers walked upstairs and joined him.

"Pop cell 3." One of the jailers said thru his radio

The door popped open. All three jailers rushed in on Justice and began beating him with their nightsticks. Justice tried everything in his power to fight back, but his efforts were fruitless. While being beaten his eyes landed on one of the Jailers name tag, he thought he recognized the man then darkness struck him as he drifted off to unconsciousness. They left him badly beaten on the floor.

Two days went by Justice was still in the hole no medical attention nor phone calls was giving as he sat battered in his cell he remembered the jailers name "Grant". He swore to himself to pay Grant back in the most violent way possible. Pacing back and forth he sat on his bunk and remembered where he recognized the jailer from. Grant was from the Bottoms. He remember seeing the crackhead jackpot mowing the yard of one of the houses that he had seen him come out of. "Yeah I got your ass now," he said out loud talking to himself. Then he became frustrated that he was still in jail and wondered why Lisa hadn't come to bond him out yet. Two more days went by. After his bruises were healed they finally let him back into population. As soon as he walked in the Block he went straight to the phone and called his girl.

'Ring', 'Ring'.

"Hello." Lisa answered on the second ring.

"Baby, why haven't you gotten me out yet?"

"I've been trying, they kept telling me you were at another jail. I didn't find out what was up until I bonded Amir out."

"So what's up?"

"I'm outside now with the Bondsmen, and your lawyer. The

Bondsman is doing the paperwork now. You'll be out in a minute."

"Okay baby, love you."

"Love you too. Just be patient we're here."

"Okay." Justice replied and then hung the phone up and sat in front of the T.V. and watched as the Cowboys played the Eagles. While sitting down taking in his surroundings he noticed that he knew a couple of the guys in the Block. Justice dapped them up and kicked it with them until his name was called.

"Justice Santiago, pack it up you've made bail." The jailer bellowed. Glancing around the cell he had called home for almost a week. He packed up *Bout time someone follow instructions* Justice thought to himself as he grabbed his mat and headed to the door.

"A yo Styles Im'a put a hundred on your books. I'll call your girl later and see what's up with bail. Tell Dez I got him too." Justice informed while heading out.

"Good luck Bruh. I'll tell Dez what you said, when he wakes up." Styles replied.

"Stunna Boys we in here." A couple guys on the top tier hollered as loud as they could as the slider door came open and Justice walked out. Finally reaching the booking desk he spotted Grant and gave him a frightening smile.

"Fuck you nigga, you ain't shit pig." Justice taunted.

"Punk ass street thug. You'll be back, and I'll be waiting on your ass." Grant spat.

"We'll see won't we?"

"God damn it Santiago sign these fucking papers and get the hell outta my jail. You little piece of shit." Sgt. Cook growled.

"You know what Sgt. Fuck you too."

"I hope for your sake your ass don't come back here boy. I don't want you to end up like your mamma. You know you can't win we're the biggest gang in the World." Sgt. Cook shot back.

"Keep my mother's name out your mouth." Justice said as he signed his release papers. Handing the pen over Justice grabbed his property, his wallet, watch, chain and a few rings, then headed out the double doors. *This nigga Grant's whole family's dead he doesn't know who he's fucking wit,* Justice thought to himself. When he finally walked out to the parking lot. The first face he saw was his sexy girlfriend Lisa. He smiled to himself knowing he had the sexiest snow bunny in the city, and she had that paper. It was nothing more sexier than a bad chick with money.

"Hey baby! I was so worried about you. Are you okay?"

"Yeah I'm good, my Caddy is totaled, but I'm ok."

"Don't worry about the car. We'll get you another one. I'm just so happy to see you. Mama gonna take good care of you when we get home."

Justice smiled as Lisa hugged him tightly.

"I'm glad this is ok." Lisa whispered reaching down and gently rubbing the bulge poking from his Levi Jeans.

"Yeah we good ma, let's get out of here." Justice replied, then headed to the passenger side of Lisa 550 Benz.

"No baby, I want you to drive. I got something for you." Lisa said as she opened the passenger door and got inside.

Seeing this Justice got in the driver side, Lisa passed him her keys. Justice crunk the car up and pulled out of the jailhouse parking lot. When they got on the interstate Lisa reached her hand over and began to rub Justices crotch until she was sure that he was good and hard.

"Keep your eyes on the road baby." Lisa said as she began to unbutton Justice's jeans letting his eight inch dick free from its silk confinement. She gently stroked him before she leaned over putting her head in his lap sucking him slowly as he drove home.

Lisa was Justice's Queen, and she loved to please her man. It was nothing she wouldn't do for him. Putting her head game down it didn't take Lisa but ten minutes to drain Justice dry, swallowing his seed as she always did because she loved the taste of him. When she finished she wiped her mouth with the back of her hand, then grabbed a paper towel out of her glove compartment. She wiped her mouth again smiling to herself while watching Justice put his dick back in his pants. Twenty minutes later Justice was pulling into the driveway of their three bedroom home, they both got out, and held each other's hand as they walked inside.

    Justice loved Lisa. They had been together for five years and had been through plenty of storms together. No matter what it was they always made it through because their love for each other was strong. The first storm came when they first got together. They had met each other at a college house party and hit it off quickly. After going on a couple dates things got serious. When it did Lisa's father didn't approve. He didn't like the fact that his baby girl was dating a black guy from the hood. He pulled Lisa to the side and had forbidden her from seeing Justice. Her father's words fell on deaf ears because Lisa snuck around to see Justice anyway. Until one day she became pregnant. She tried to hide her pregnancy for months but her father eventually found out and became angry that his baby girl was having a baby by a black man. Being a wealthy lawyer at a huge law firm. He felt his daughter would be an embarrassment. He was so angry, and humiliated that he gave her a hundred and fifty thousand dollars and told her that he never wanted to see her again. The money was transferred to her account, but she had nowhere to stay. Lisa went straight to Justice who was staying with his grandmother at the time. Saddened by her situation Vidah Santiago gave Justice her blessing, and he took her in with open arms, wiped the tears away from her eyes and told her everything would be okay.

    Grateful that her man had her back she told Justice about the money that her father had given her. Justice was a street nigga, his mother had taught him the game before she died of cancer. He took fifty thousand, and hit the streets building himself a team along with his best friend Amir. In just a few months Justice and his Stunna Boys had taken the streets over. Money was coming in so fast from the guns he was selling that they bought a three bedroom house on the outskirts of Chapel Hill. The house sat on three acres of land. As time went by their good days became dark and cloudy. Lisa had given birth to a baby boy that they had named Pharell after Justice's mother Danielle. The baby was born premature, and had trouble breathing. Baby Pharell ended up passing away eight weeks after he was born. His death was a trying time for Justice and Lisa, but it brought them even closer. They formed an unbreakable bond. From that point it was them against the World. Even after the baby passed Lisa never went back to her father.

Chapter 2

Money Time

After making bond, and chilling with his girl, Justice reached out to Amir to see what was up. He sauntered out the patio, and pulled out his cell phone, and called Amir.

'Ring, Ring'.

"Justice what up Bro?" Amir answered after looking at his caller I.D.

"Not too much. Just got through chillen with Lisa. You close by?"

"Yeah, I'm on the Dirt Road doing what I do best."

Justice chuckled knowing his partner was in the hood trapping.

"Yo, I doubled back and got that after Lisa made my bond." Amir informed.

"Good that's what's up. Look, stay put. I'm on my way over

there now. I got something I need cleaned up."

"Facts I'll be here."

"Aite one." Justice retorted, hanging his phone up, and placing it back in his pocket as he walked back inside.

When he went in Lisa was in the kitchen naked making a couple of omelets. Justice stopped briefly and admired her sexy body. Lisa looked up from the stove and caught him staring, and smiled.

"What is it baby?"

"Nothing just admiring the view." Justice replied as he strolled into the kitchen making his way behind Lisa, then lightly grabbing her by the waist.

"I gotta make a run real quick, and check on Amir."

"Don't you wanta eat first?" Lisa asked, as she picked up the pan, and put the two omelets on a plate.

"Put it in the microwave for me. I'll eat it when I get back."

Lisa smiled and giggled.

"What is it baby?"

"I know you gotta handle your business, but it feels like this isn't ready for you to leave just yet." Lisa retorted reaching her hand behind her and rubbing her man's penis through his jeans.

"You might be right." Justice said as he began to unbuckle his belt.

"You wanta go back to the bedroom for round two?"

"No baby. I want it right here." Justice replied letting his jeans fall to the floor then he rubbed his dick gently up and down the crack of Lisa's ass.

"Baby the food."

"Fuck the food." Justice whispered as he slowly bent Lisa over the stove, and entered her from behind.

"Baby you're so nasty."

"I know, that's why you love me so much." Justice said as he began to slide in and out of Lisa's wet pink pussy.

"Aaah babbby aargh aah ahh." Lisa moaned as Justice grabbed both of her wrist, and held them like handle bars, as she took every inch of him from behind.

"I-I-I Love you Aaah."

"I love you too." Justice retorted through grunts as he continued to pound.

"Aaah baby, I'm coming Justice."

"Cum for me, cum for daddy."

"Aaaaaaah." Lisa moaned as she released covering Justice's dick with her juices. Seconds later Justice busted all in Lisa's love box. Catching her breath.

"You trying to get me pregnant?" Lisa asked.

"You know it. I need me a lil man or a lil Lisa running around." Justice replied as he pulled out and grabbed a paper towel, and wiped his dick off, pulling up his pants he buckled his belt, then turned Lisa around and gave her a kiss.

"I gotta go."

"Okay baby please be careful."

"I will baby. No worries."

"Okay."

Justice headed out the door, and hopped in his Suburban, and pulled out of the driveway headed to the Dirt Road to meet Amir. Pulling up at the Dirt Road surrounded by old junk cars, and run down houses. Amir, and his partner Harlem World was sitting on the porch smoking a blunt enjoying the summer breeze.

Justice hopped out of his truck and winced as a slight pain shot up his shoulders. His arm was still in a sling. He tried to hide his pain as he walked up on the front porch, and saluted his comrades.

"Yo what's good?" Justice asked.

"You already know, Stunna Boys." Harlem World retorted.

Justice smiled at the young hustler "Sho nuff." Justice shot back.

"Yo bro that wreck fucked you up huh, here goes your hammer. I went back, and got em the day after Lisa posted my bond." Amir said handing Justice his tool. He took it with a sly grin. Knowing he was ready to use it to pay Grant back for what he did to him in the county.

"Yeah I dislocated my shoulder. I'm good tho. No pain no gain feel me?"

"Yeah, Bruh you know I know."

"I got into it with Bruno from the Bottoms. He thought he was going to get off because my shoulder was fucked up. I ran into Murder Tone and we took care of that shit."

"You talking about Tone, Tone. Stunna boy Tone?" Amir asked.

"Yeah we fucked around and jumped Bruno, fucked him up pretty good before the jailers came rushing in."

"You good though right?" Harlem World asked.

"Hell nah. Mutha fuckas hit me with that stun gun, and threw me in the hole which would have been fine, but the jailer Grant he's from the Bottoms to. Him and his goons ran in my cell."

"What you mean ran in your cell?" Amir asked.

"They fucked me up pretty good, then left me. They wouldn't bring me my mail or send my letters out, then he had his staff to tell Lisa I wasn't there when she came to try to bond me out."

"So that's what took you so long to get out?"

"Yeah Im'a murk that nigga for that shit."

"Nah Big homie! I think I know the dude you're speaking about. Grant from the Bottoms." Harlem World pondered. "Yeah that fools name is Marcus, he a police ass nigga. I've been wanting to roll on him. Let me handle that for you?" Harlem asked.

"Nah it's kinda personal lil Bruh. Im'a make this dude feel me too."

"I can't let you do that with that banged up shoulder of yours." Harlem World replied unrelenting in his statement.

"He's right Justice. We need you out here, and focused. We got money to make." Amir stated trying to bring Justice to his senses.

"Aite then kill his wife, and burn her beauty shop to the ground. I'll handle Marcus when I heal up." Justice spat angrily at himself for being hurt.

"Bet it's still early. I'll handle that shit today, on Stunna I got cha." Harlem World replied, then got up from where he was sitting, and dapped his partners up. Hopping in his 64 Impala Harlem pulled off focused on his mission, and earning a few more stripes.

Justice and Amir watched as Harlem World cruised down the street until his tail lights were out of sight.

"Baby boy still trying to put in work?" Justice stated.

"He be on his New York shit. You already know how he is." Amir answered.

"Live wire. I got mad love for the Bro tho."

Seeing Harlem as they both walked inside the old house. It was time to re-up.

"Yo bro grab the duffle out of the basement so we can count this week's revenue."

As ordered Amir walked down into the basement and retrieved the duffle bag that was hidden inside an old piano that Amir's grandmother used to play for him when he was little. The house they were in wasn't abandoned it had belonged to Amir's grandmother, as well as four other houses that were located on the Dirt Road. The land belonged to his family, but everything was left to his older sister Jenny, who didn't care much for the property. She stayed out in Florida with some football player, and almost never came to Chapel Hill let alone North Carolina period. It didn't matter if Jenny came home or not, he always made sure all of the family affairs were in order. After securing the bag Amir walked back upstairs to the living room and dropped the bag on the floor next to Justices feet. Whom quickly squatted and opened the bag pulling out two medium size money machines then sat them on the table. Justice and Amir both began removing stacks of money out of the duffle bag and ran them through the money machines one stack at a time. It took them almost an hour to finish running all of the money. Two hundred and fifty thousand all rubber banded in stacks of ten thousand.

After everything was accounted for Justice pulled out his phone and called his plug.

'Ring', 'Ring'.
"Speak." The plug said.
"I'm ready."
"You know where to find me. What's the number?" the plug asked.
"Two hundred and fifty."
"Good, Good. I see business is good. Call me when you get close by."
"I got cha. I'm on my way now." Justice replied, before hanging his phone up. "Come on let's get this money packed back up. I got a five hour drive ahead of me. I need to hit the road quick."
"Bruh you sure you wanta drive the Atlanta with all this money, wit your arm hanging in a sling?" Amir asked concerned about his friend's wellbeing.
"I'm good this here is baby money to these guys. Im'a shoot down there, and snatch these hammers up, then we going to fill these orders and get this money. No worries bro. Trust a G on that." Justice replied.
"I trust you Bro, you know that. It's the guys you're meeting that I don't trust."
"Big risk big gain, stop being so damn paranoid. I've been dealing with Phatom for years. Come on man put that money in the truck so I can hit the road." Justice ordered.
Amir did as he was asked, then they dapped each other up with brotherly love, then Justice climbed inside his truck and pulled off.

Harlem World was down for all that murder shit, and he loved using his imagination while doing it. When he was back in New York that's all he did was drop bodies with his murder unit team. A bunch of up top guns for hire, who didn't mind snatching souls for that almighty dollar. He hated to leave his team, but currently he was on the run for killing a crooked judge who sentenced one of his comrades to a life sentence, that's the only reason he was even in North Carolina, otherwise he wouldn't be caught dead down here with these country niggas. Truth of the matter tho he fucked with Amir and Justice the long way. They were about that money, and they kept food on his plate, and really at this point in his life that's all that mattered to him. Right now he had to put in this work, and he would make sure it was pretty work. He knew when the job was done Justice would bless him real nice. Currently he was putting his imagination to use as he wiped fresh white face paint all over his face. When he finished he placed a red ball over his nose, transforming himself into the soft version of It the killer clown. Satisfied with his disguise he grabbed the forty balloons that he had spent a half hour blowing up. Holding the balloons Harlem World smiled at himself in the mirror doing a double take to make sure everything was to his liking before leaving out. Satisfied he headed out the door, and jumped inside an old stolen Saturn that he had kept in the cut for times like this.

It took Harlem World roughly forty-five minutes to get to Greensboro where Grant's wife Sarah owned a beauty shop. He parked two streets over, then reached inside his glove compartment, and pulled out a small long barrel thirty eight special old western revolver, he tucked it inside his clown suit grabbed the balloons out of the backseat, then he exited the stolen Sudan. Looking around making sure he didn't look out of place, he opened the trunk and pulled out a small cart that had more balloons that he had twisted up and made to look like animals. It was also a small jug of gasoline hidden deep under the balloons and his bag of tricks that he would use to attract kids as he watched the beauty shop until it was the right time to strike. Shutting the trunk Harlem World began to push his cart up the street making honking sounds with his nose, as he passed out balloons to the children that came his way. He worked his way all the way up Lee Street, where Grant's wife's beauty shop was located. When he spotted the place he was looking for he set up shop, and began to work his magic, as he made jokes and passed out balloons to passer byers, and people coming out of the beauty shop.

Harlem World worked the crowd for hours as people gathered around. He had even walked inside the beauty shop a couple of times to get water whenever he became thirsty. It was now 5:30 pm all of Grants wife's customers left but she was still inside alone cleaning her shop, and preparing to close. Seeing that this was the right time to strike Harlem World eased himself inside with the silence of a predator stalking his prey.

Finally inside Grant's wife came walking from the back pushing a mop bucket. When she looked up she was shocked at Harlem World's sudden presence.

"I'm sorry ma'am, I didn't mean to scare you." Harlem World said trying to calm her nerves.

"Oh it's okay. I'm just kinda in a rush to get this place clean so I can get home to my husband and mommy duties."

"I understand, I have a family at home too. Here take a balloon." Harlem World replied as he held out his hand to give Grant's wife a couple of balloons. Feeling at ease Sarah put the mop back inside the bucket, and then walked over, and reached for the balloons smiling from ear to ear. Harlem World pulled the revolver that he had hidden behind his back, before Sarah knew what was happening. Harlem World pulled the trigger shooting her in the face splattering blood everywhere. He then picked her lifeless body up, and sat her in one of the shops beauty chairs. Smiling to himself he grabbed a comb out of one of the drawers, and began to comb her hair. Reaching in his pocket he pulled out a red tube of make-up and proceeded to draw a smile on her face. Satisfied he retrieved the can of gasoline that he had hidden in his cart. Taking a second look Harlem World laughed to himself as he pours gasoline all around her shop, then he walked out the door and lit a match setting the whole shop ablaze. Once he hit the sidewalk he took off in a light jog, continuing his pace until he reached the old stolen Saturn. Jumping inside Harlem slammed the door, crunk the car up and pulled off heading to the highway.

When Harlem World got back to Chapel Hill, he walked into his spot and began removing his face paint and his clown costume. He packed everything away inside a duffel bag, and slid the bag it under his bed.

After he cleaned himself up, he remembered that Marcus had a brother named Omar that stay in the Bottoms next to the old train station. *I think Justice would appreciate it if I reached out and touched him too*, Harlem World thought to himself as he looked in the mirror. Walking out of the bathroom Harlem got dressed then grabbed the old thirty-eight that he killed Grant's wife with off the bed tucking it inside his pants. He wiped the sweat from his forehead with the palm of his hand. He knew he had a problem. Once he started laying his murder game down it was hard for him to cut it off that's the reason he was on the run, and had to leave his murder unit click. Without thinking twice he grabbed his motorcycle helmet off the coffee table, and headed back out the door with nothing but murder on his mind. He hopped on his Suzuki Hayabusa, stuck his key in and crunk her up. He placed his venom looking helmet on over his head, then smacked the throttle letting the monster roar right before he put the bike in gear, and pulled off.

Speeding down the side roads Harlem World's adrenaline pumped as he leaned on the throttle pushing the bike to 120 mph. When he got to his destination he cut his bike off, and rolled it inside a path deep in the woods. He kicked the kickstand out, and sat his bike down. He took off his helmet and sat it on the tank, then he took his key out of the ignition and opened his seat and pulled out a black ski-mask that he always kept. He pulled it over his face, it fit perfectly tight concealing all of his facial features, then he continued to walk thru the woods until he came to the old train station where there was nothing but old abandoned train cars. Harlem continued to walk all the way through to the other side of the path. When it opened up Marcus brother's house was in clear view. He check his watch it was 9:00pm. He walked through Omar's yard, and spotted a light on in the garage, slowly he plodded towards it. Seeing a window open he stepped up on the same old truck tanks and looked inside. Instantly he spotted Omar standing under his old Cutlass doing some work on the transmission while drinking a beer.

    The Cutlass was held high in the air on a car lift. *This would be easy.* Harlem World thought to himself as he climbed down, and eased his way inside the wide open door of Omar's shop. He looked around until he spotted what he was looking for, which was the lever button to the car lift. Slowly he walked over to it making his presence known right before he pushed the button. The Cutlass dropped right on top of Omar crushing him and killing him. Harlem World pulled the old revolver out of his waistline. Looking around he found an old work rag laying on the floor. He picked it up and wiped his finger prints off the gun that he had just killed Marcus wife with. He placed it in Omar's dead hands making sure his finger prints were all over the murder weapon, then he removed it from his hand using the work rag he walked over and sat the gun on the table next to Omar's beer. This was not expected nor in his plans, but it would work. It would look like Omar killed Sarah Grant, and not Justice nor himself. "I love it when a plan comes together," Harlem World says out loud to himself, as he walked out of the shop and disappeared into the darkness, as he headed back thru the woods to his bike. No one would ever know he was even there.

Chapter 3

The Next Day

When Justice returned from his business trip to Atlanta. He was carrying a crate of fully automatic AR-15's. Needless to say he went straight to his destination which was Chapel Hill. After the nervous ride back he was finally pulling onto the Dirt Road. Amir met him at the top on two dirt bikes. Seeing them waiting Justice stopped and checked the two riders to make sure they were his comrades. Content with his assessment Justice drove past them so they could follow him in.

After he parked Amir took off his helmet, and signaled to Red Bull which was the second rider to unload Justices truck. Red Bull nodded before setting himself upon his task.

Justice and Amir both walked inside.

"Glad to see you made it back, I get nervous every time you make the trip." Amir confessed.

"You shouldn't. I told you, I'm good."

"Anything could happen tho."

"I know, but Phatom always has his people follow me back until I reach Charlotte. I'm on my own from there."

"That's what I'm worried about."

"I'll tell you what from now on. I want you and Harlem World to meet me in Charlotte. Ya'll can follow me the rest of the way. Get Red Bull and Halftime to check the perimeter to make sure we don't have any Sheriffs hanging out in the woods on us."

"I'm on it. Speaking of Harlem World. He took care of that for you." Amir replied handing Justice two newspapers, one for Greensboro and the other from Chapel Hill. Justice grabbed the newspapers and sat down as he began to read.

He quickly stumbled on what he was looking for.

Beauty shop burnt down confirmed one dead Mrs. Sarah Grant, married to Marcus Grant. Justice smiled seeing all he needed to see closing the paper he opened up the Chapel Hill paper and was surprised when he saw Marcus brother Omar on the front page. It looked like a car had fell on him. Reading the article further, he came across a line that said murder weapon found. He didn't quite understand, so he looked up at Amir.

"What is this?" Justice asks.

"What you mean." Amir questioned, "My boy is a fool wit it."

"Harlem shot Sarah, and burnt the shop down like you asked, then he went and killed Marcus's brother, and planted the murder weapon on him, so nothing would lead back to us." Amir replied.

"What the fuck. I mean shit, I didn't know Harlem could think like that. Let's wrap this up here. I need to go see the Bro. I gotta make sure I bless him real nice." Just as Justice began to relax Red Bull walked in the backdoor.

"Everything is unloaded Big Bro." Red bull informed.

"Good, good is everything secured?"

"Of course, unless you want me to bust the crates open?" Red Bull replied.

"No I'll do that later myself." Justice said, as he got up and walked downstairs to the basement. He went to the small safe that him and Amir kept for the crew. Opened the digital dial and punched in the code. The safe clicked, and the door popped open. Justice reached in and grabbed two large stacks then shut the door back, and walked back upstairs, after shutting the basement door.

"Keep a eye on things here, Red Bull get a hold of Halftime, I want you both to set up your plays for moving the weapons. I know you're tight with the Sur-13 in Durham. See what they need. Amir, ride with me let's go see Harlem World."

"Aite Bruh, I'll take care of things here, and make a few calls." Red Bull replied dapping Justice and Amir up, then he watched them head out the door.

Justice and Amir hopped in Justice's black Suburban and pulled off heading to see Harlem World. It didn't take them but ten minutes to get to Harlem's spot since it was really up the road. When they pulled up, they immediately knew Harlem was at home, because they spotted his Impala parked in the driveway. Justice pulled right up beside it, and him and Amir hopped out, and walked up on the porch, and knocked on the old screen door. After three knocks Harlem World peeked out the door.

"It's me, and Amir bro open up." Justice says announcing himself.

Harlem World opened the door. When he did Justice looked down, and noticed that Harlem was holding a nine millimeter in his hand.

"What's up Bro? Damn what's that for?"

"You can never be too sure plus you guys were knocking like the police." Harlem World replied.

"My bad Bro."

"You good come on inside." Harlem said opening the door letting his Bros in.

"Have a seat. I'll put this Madden on and bust ya'll ass if you want to play?" Harlem asked.

"Naw we good on that." Amir replied, as he and Justice sat down on the couch.

"Make yourselves at home. Want something to drink. I got a little Henny in the cabinet." Harlem asked.

"Yeah, let me get a shot on the rocks." Justice answered.

"Aite, and you Amir?"

"I'm good bruh, it's against my faith."

"Damn I forgot my bad."

"You good." Amir replied.

"You want some water."

"I'm okay Bruh."

"Aite, then." Harlem said as he disappeared into the kitchen, and returned with two shots of Henny in his hand. He handed one to Justice and he gulped the other.

"That was a good job that you did. I'm very impressed." Justice said giving Harlem his props.

"It was nothing Bro anything for the team. Mutha fuckers disrespect you is like them disrespecting me. It's off with their head feel me. You don't have to worry about anything coming back. I went ahead and took care of that too."

"I see, I read the papers." Justice retorted reaching inside his coat pocket. He grabbed the two stacks of money that he had retrieved from the crews safe and handed them both to Harlem. "This is for your troubles, and expenses." Justice said. Harlem grabbed the money, and sat it on his bookshelf.

"How much is it?" Harlem asked.

"Thirty thousand, is that good?"

"Big Bro that's more than enough. I would've done it for free, you and Amir are my peoples feel me?"

Amir slightly grinned at Harlem, loving how his young goon gave it up.

"I know you would've, but it's just in me. I look out for all my peoples. Everybody on my team eats."

"I feel it bro, and I do appreciate it. Just let me know if you need me again, and I'm there no questions asked."

"That's what I like to hear." Justice replied as he stood up and gulped down his shot and then dapped Harlem up.

"Stunna Boys."

"For life." Harlem replied.

Justice walked out the door headed back to his truck. Amir hung back wanting to say a few things to Harlem since in reality Harlem was Amir's prospect. After about five minutes Amir came walking out with a smile on his face. He got in the truck and Justice pulled off.

In wake of dropping Amir off on the Dirt Road so he could link up with Red Bull and Halftime. Justice headed home since he had already been out too late, and he knew Lisa was probably worried about him, like she always did when he went out to handle his business. He was surprised that she wasn't blowing his phone up. Checking his Rolex he seen that it was 5:30pm. Pulling into the driveway of his three bedroom house, he got out and walked inside. He had been gone since yesterday so he knew Lisa was inside waiting for him. Justice was tired and wanted to rest, but he knew that she would want to get out of the house for a little while.

When Justice walked inside Lisa was sitting in their Livingroom watching soaps probably Young and the Restless or As the World Turns. He didn't know or cared which, she liked them, and that was good enough for him.

"Hey baby." Justice says, as he walked inside the living room, and bent over and kissed Lisa on her cheek.

"Hey I was worried about you."

"No need to worry baby."

"I'm always worried about you. Especially when you go on your overnight trips." Lisa replied as she rubbed Justices arm, then pulled him down on the couch.

"I know you have to handle your business but I always worry." Lisa confessed.

"After I save up enough money for us to live off of Im'a quit and let Amir take over."

"You always say that. Just don't get caught up baby. Nothing lasts forever." Lisa replied.

"We last forever, me and you."

"I love you too." Lisa smiled.

"I know you've been in the house all day, I need to go see my grandma. She said she had something to talk to me about. You wanta ride with me?"

"Yeah baby I'll ride with you. Let me go upstairs and get ready." Lisa replied as she got up from the couch and headed upstairs.

Siler City

"Hey Grandma."

"Hey baby, how have you been?"

"Fine grandma."

"I see you brought your other half with you."

"How are you Mrs. Santiago?" Lisa said as she walked over and gave Justices grandma a hug.

"I'm okay, I see you've been taking care of my grandson. He's put on a little weight. You aren't cooking him any fried foods are you?" Mrs. Santiago asked.

Lisa smiled.

"No grandma. I try to lay off the salt and cook healthy foods for him."

"His mother always loved fried chicken and okra."

"Grandma." Justice tried to protest.

"Oh hush baby. Come on in the den. I have something I need to tell you." Mrs. Santiago replied as she led the way thru her house to her den. Justice and Lisa sat on the couch and watched as his grandma walked into her room, and grabbed a picture fame off of her dresser then she strolled back in and sat in her old recliner.

"Whose picture is that grandma?" Justice asked.

Mrs. Santiago sighed as she began to remove the weight from

her shoulder that she had carried for 37 years. She handed Justice the picture frame.

Grabbing it Justice asked, "Who is this grandma."

"That is your older brother, his name is Kanden."

Justice looked at the picture closely. The guy was light skin, stocky with big dreads, and brown eyes. He looked like an older version of himself.

"What do you mean this is my brother grandma?"

"Your mother had a son before she met your father by one of your father's friends." Mrs. Santiago informed.

"Why didn't mama tell me about him?"

"Kanden's father was murdered, there were rumors that your mother was responsible for his death but nothing was ever proven. Kanden's father stole him from Danielle and hid him when your mother refused to leave your father. Kanden's father refused to return Kanden to your mother, after your father requested it. Months later Kanden's father disappeared. I believe your father fed him to the pigs. After his disappearance your mother closed that door behind her when she gave birth to you and your sister."

"Does Zeenah know about him grandma?" Justice asked.

"Lord no, I want her to focus on school and basketball. If Zeenah knew about Kanden she would be out trying to find him. You're the only one that knows besides me and your father."

"Grandma why are you just now telling me about him?"

"Kanden called, and wanted me to tell you about him. His phone number is written on the back of the picture."

Justice handed the picture frame to Lisa, and she opened it, and took the picture out, then handed it to Justice, whom looked at the number and then at his grandmother.

"I can't believe you kept this from us grandma." Justice said, as he placed his face in his hands.

"I'm so sorry baby, but after losing your mother to cancer when she was sent to prison I didn't want to open these wounds back up. Your brother is fighting his own battle with cancer this may be why he wants to meet you after all these years."

"Grandma are you serious?" Justice asked as Lisa leaned over and hugged him.

"I am baby." Mrs. Santiago confirmed.

"What am I supposed to do, this is a lot of weight coming at me all at once."

"Call him Justice go and see him. He's your brother, my daughter's son. Your mother would want you to go to him."

"After all these years grandma. I wouldn't even know what to say to him. Does he need money?"

"No grandson your brother is wealthy. He needs nothing from us. Go see him. We will not talk about this anymore do as your grandmother says."

Justice could hear the frustration in his grandmother's voice, and he knew very well what could happen if he angered her, he just needed answers, and he knew he had to meet Kanden to get them.

"I will do as you say grandma, but I have one more question."

"What is it son?" Mrs. Santiago asked.

"My mother died inside of a prison hospital. Did she ever get a chance to speak with Kanden before she died?"

"Your mother longed to talk to Kanden, but she didn't get a chance. Danielle died not knowing what her son had become. This is why you must go see him."

"I will grandma I promise."

"You better or you are not welcome here any longer. Now with that said you, and Lisa go to the dining table so you can eat with an old lady. I made baked chicken, green beans, and mashed potatoes, and gravy. Zeenah will be back from the gym soon. I don't want you leaving without seeing your sister."

"Yes grandma, come on baby." Justice said to Lisa as he stood up and headed to the dining room. Sitting at the table side by side Mrs. Santiago brought in the dinner plates, and set the table. Justice tapped Lisa on her leg letting her know to go in the kitchen and help his grandmother. By the time both women set the table with mama Santiago's soul food Zeenah was coming through the front door bouncing a basketball.

"Stop bouncing that ball in the house young lady." Mrs. Santiago hollered from the kitchen.

"Okay grandma." Zeenah hollered back as she picked up the ball and held it under her arms.

Justice got up from the table and walked over and hugged his sister.

"Aah Justice don't squeeze me to death."

"I can't help it sis you know how much I love you." Justice said chuckling.

"How have you been Zeenah?" Justice asked.

"Basketball, basketball, and more basketball other than that I'm okay. How about you?"

"I'm good sis."

"Come on what is it. I can always tell when something's wrong with you." Zeenah stated.

"I got somethings on my mind, but nothing to serious tho. I'm good it ain't nothing big Bro can't handle."

"Yeah, I know you think you're superman. But you can always come talk to me."

"I know sis, I know enough about me. What college are you going to Florida, Duke, Chapel Hill or Clemson?"

"I don't know yet. It's a surprise you gotta come to my signing day to find out."

"I wouldn't miss it for the World. Lisa wants to come is that okay?"

"Yeah, that's fine she's family too. Where is she anyway?"

"In the kitchen with grandma. Zeenah you know I want you to come to Chapel Hill so we can be close."

"Come to my signing day. You'll know what I choose then. Enough about basketball for now, I'm hungry." Zeenah replied.

"Just like grandma always telling me what to do." Justice replied then shook his head and returned to his seat at the table.

Mrs. Santiago and Lisa emerged from the kitchen with the food, then they all sat and ate enjoying each other's company.

After eating they all sat and talked while Mrs. Santiago watched her wrestling, and cheered for her favorite wrestler Ray Mistero.

Chapter 4

Committed

Thursday 3:20 pm. Justice, Lisa and mama Santiago stood behind Zeenah Santiago on her college commitment day at JM High School. Zeenah Santiago was among the top ten national recruits coming out of high school. She ranked number two in the nation averaging forty points a game. Zeenah sat at a table that was set up for her in the lobby. She had many scholarship offers, but currently only had four of the top schools hats on the table in front of her to choose from which were Chapel Hill, Connecticut Huskies, Duke, and Oregon Ducks. Lights and cameras flashed as she made her decision. Zeenah looked at her brother Justice, as she waved her hand over all four hats. She smiled then grabbed the Carolina Blue UNC Tarheels hat off the table, and placed it on her head. Cameras went flashing as Channel 8 news took pictures of the most talented female athlete coming out of the state of North Carolina. Everyone was

pleased that the talent would stay in its home state. Most of all Mrs. Santiago, and Justice were very happy, and proud of their granddaughter and sister. When everything was over the news station took pictures of Zeenah Santiago and her family.

"I'm so proud of you, and your mother would be proud of you too." Mrs. Santiago said.

"I know grandma everything I do is for you and her. I know she's looking down watching over us." Zeenah replied.

"We're proud of you too." Justice said as him and Lisa hugged his little sister.

"I know you are Justice."

"Sis what made you pick UNC? I know you wanted to go to Connecticut and win a championship."

"Yeah, but what would I look like leaving you all by yourself. Lisa will definitely need a break. Besides I know you wanted me to come to Chapel Hill, and I can win a championship at UNC, they have a good program there, and plus the family will be able to come to all my home games." Zeenah replied.

"You already know we'll be there." Lisa chuckled.

After the college day signing they all went out to eat at Outback Steakhouse to celebrate. When they finished eating Justice and Lisa dropped Zeenah and Mrs. Santiago off at home then they returned to Chapel Hill.

When they finally got home Justice was exhausted he went straight to the shower to try to relieve some of the stress that he was under at finding out after all these years that he had an older brother, and the fact that he was sick hurt him even more. As Justice undressed, he stepped in the shower and let the warm water wash away his pain. When he turned around he noticed Lisa was stepping in behind him.

"Do you mind if I join you?" Lisa said smiling flashing her pearly whites.

"No baby you're okay." Justice turned around and began to roughly kiss Lisa pushing her back towards the shower wall, then he began kissing her neck moving slowly to her breast. Lisa moaned from the pleasure she was receiving. Slowly Justice lowered himself until he was face was inches from her pussy lifting her right leg he began to taste her honey pot. Lisa braced her hands on the wall as he man took her to another world.

"Aaaaah I'm cumming." She moaned releasing her juices in Justices mouth, and on his face. Before Justice stood up he let the water run over his face, then he stood lifting Lisa up in the process. He held her leg eagle with her back against the wall. He entered her slowly, letting her get the feel of him. When he was sure she was ready he sped up and set about releasing his frustration on her pussy fucking her harder, and harder. Lisa dug her nails in his back, as she screamed in pleasure, and pain. Justice let her down, and quickly flipped her over. Lisa gripped the wall, Justice pulled her blond hair as he entered her from behind and embarked on pounding her back out. Nothing could be heard but grunts and moans and the slapping of skin as Justice spread her cheeks.

"Fuck me aaaah, fuck me baby."

"Whose pussy is this?"

"It's yours baby it's yours."

He grunted releasing his seed inside his Queen. When he pulled out, Lisa turned around and stroked his penis as she kissed the man that she loved so deeply. She took her wash cloth and lathered it with soap and began to wash his chest. When they finished bathing each other and drying off Justice and Lisa laid naked on the bedside side by side. She rubbed his chest and played with his nipple until he was hard all over again.

"I think you should call your brother."

"I don't know baby."

"He's family baby, and you never turn your back on family, ain't that what you always preach to me."

"I know, but this is different."

"No it's not, and you already promised grandma. If you don't call, you won't get any more of this." Lisa replied as she slid down and kissed the head of Justices dick, the she looked up and smiled at him as she place his penis in her mouth and commence to sucking him slowly. Leaning his head back he closed his eyes and enjoyed the pleasure his girl was giving him. After he released in her mouth, she cleaned him up and they both got dressed. While watching T.V. Justice took heed to what his grandma had said. He had already memorized his brother's number, so he picked up his phone and dialed Kanden's number.

Ring, Ring, Ring.

"Hello." Kanden answered.

"What's up? This is-."

"I know who this is. How are you doing Justice?" Kanden asked.

"I'm good man, what about you?"

"I'm good."

"I know grandma has already told you a little bit about me, but it's important that I speak with you in person. Can we meet?"

"Yeah where?" Justice asked.

"I own a bar in Burlington called Dragon's Bar + Grill on Huffman Mill Road meet me there in one hour."

"One hour it is. See you soon." Justice answered.

When Justice hung up the phone, he looked up and saw that Lisa was standing right behind him with a smile on her face.

"I knew you would call. How did it go?" Lisa asked.

"It was short, and to the point. He wants me to meet him at Dragon's Bar and Grill."

"You want me to ride with you?" Lisa asked trying to show her support.

"No I got it baby this is something I have to do myself." Justice replied as he got up and grabbed his keys off the coffee table, and gave Lisa a hug before he headed out the door.

Amir and Red Bull loaded Amir's truck with a small crate of AR-15's then headed up I-85 to Durham to meet some of his

Mexican friends. Every time a fresh shipment came in Torres was always at the top of the list. One thing for sure Torres always kept that work and them guns on deck whether his crew needed them or not. It was a must to stay strapped.

After a slow forty-five minute drive they finally bared off the Durham exit. Another twenty minutes they were pulling into an old trailer park. You could tell by the car parked in the driveways that nothing but Mexicans stayed in these trailers. Amir pulled all the way to the bottom of the trailer park, pulled into the driveway of the trailer, and pulled out his phone and called Torres.

Ring, Ring.

"Hola." Torres answered.

"Hola my friend. I'm outside."

"I'm on my way now." Torres replied.

Amir hung up the phone, and let Red Bull know that Torres was on the way out. Being that this was Red Bull's first trip with Amir. He pulled out his Glock 9 reading himself for the quick exchange.

"What you think you're doing with that." Amir asked.

"Staying ready."

"Man do you know where the fuck we're at. This is little Mexico it's nothing but Mexicans out here."

"So what."

"Muthafucka here they come, put that shit away before you get us both killed." Amir replied. Hopping out of the truck as he walked over to greet Torres.

Taking Amir's advice Red Bull put his gun away tucking it in his pants before he got out. Opening the door he got out and walked to the back of the truck and stood like a statue.

"Hola, como estas." Torres said greeting Amir.

"Bien, y tu."

"Bien, who's your friend?" Torres asked pointing at Red Bull standing behind Amir's truck.

"Oh that's my partner Red Bull don't pay him no mind. It's his first time riding with me." Amir informed trying to ease any tension Torres may have had.

"I see." Torres said as he walked over to Red Bull and stuck his hand out.

"Me llamo Torres."

Red Bull shook his hand, and told him his name. Amir walked over and padded Torres on the shoulder, then he unlocked his truck tailgate, and slid the small crate out then took a small crowbar, and cracked it open.

Torres looked inside. "Nice Señor these are better than the last ones you brought me." Torres said lifting one of the AR's out of the crate pointing it in the air and examined it before placing it back inside the crate. He looked over to the Mexican that stood behind him. Snapping his fingers he point to Amir. The Mexican immediately walked over and handed Amir the shoebox he was holding under his arm.

Amir peeked inside the shoe box. A smile instantly appeared on his face as he stepped aside, and let the Mexican that handed him the shoebox unload the crates from his truck.

"Good doing business with you." Torres said dapping Amir up.

"Always my friend."

"I like your boy give him a big tip for me." Torres said as he winked his eye at Red Bull and smiled.

Red Bull returned the gesture, as he watched Torres and the other Mexicans carry the crate inside the trailer.

"Come on man let's go before you get me killed out here." Amir said to Red Bull, then they both jumped back in Amir's truck and pulled off.

After a forty-five minute drive Justice made a right turn on Huffman Mill Road pulling into the parking lot of Dragons Bar and Grill. He parked Lisa's Benz and slowly got out of the car taking a deep breath before he shut the door. Not knowing what to expect he gathered his thoughts then walked inside the bar.

Once inside it was like he was in another world. He felt like he was in China somewhere. There were stone dragons that stood like statues there were numerous pictures of Bruce Lee, and Chuck Norris that hung on the walls. Justice continued to look around as he saw more pictures that looked like an older version of himself. The guy was light skinned, stocky and he held a ninja sword in a Kung-Fu stance. This couldn't be his older brother Justice thought to himself. Deep down he knew it was.

"That was me four years ago, when I still had my strength." Kanden said.

Justice turned around to see who was speaking to him. He was caught off guard when he saw that it was his brother. He looked the same as he did in the picture that his grandma had showed him, but in person the man looked weak. He had lost a lot of weight, and walked with a cane.

"I see you're surprised by my appearance." Kanden said.

"Grandma told me you were sick."

"Yes, I have cancer. This picture here." Kanden said as he pointed to the picture of him holding a ninja sword. "I was in Japan training in this picture here, they really worked me hard, brought things outta me I didn't know I had inside."

"What made you want to get into this type of stuff?" Justice asked.

"I always enjoyed Karate, and Kung-Fu since I was a little boy. I always idolized Bruce Lee, Jim Kelly, Chuck Norris. I started training when I was twelve to keep my mind off other things that were going on in my life. When I found out I was sick I pushed my body to its limits. Kung-Fu became a obsession for me until it was time for me to take over the family business." Kanden replied as he drifted off into memory lane.

"Tell me, why is it that you wanted to meet me now after all these years?" Justice asked.

"Follow me to my office, Justice. We will speak of the business out of earshot."

Justice followed his brother, but as he followed he noticed that it hurt Kanden to walk, but he didn't say a word because he knew it would probably hurt his brother's pride.

When they got to the back office Kanden took a seat behind a huge oak desk and sat his cane close by then he motioned for Justice to have a seat.

"I called on you because I'm dying and you are my closest kin. The history between our fathers is what stopped me from contacting you sooner for fear of not knowing how our relationship would turn out."

"I have nothing to do with my father's past. I barely know him myself. He's been locked up for years." Justice replied.

"I know good and well where he is. I would have had him killed if it wasn't for grandma. She is the real controller of our family and has been for years."

"She never told me that."

"Of course she didn't, you were mama's golden child. She didn't want you in this life. She gave you a choice where I didn't have one."

"Do you fault me for that?" Justice asked.

"No brother I do not, but let us get down to business."

"Good, because I'm not used to all of this brotherly love stuff." Justice spat.

Kanden smiled. "Me either, and you're right I didn't call you for nothing. I know about your lil gun trafficking business, and I know about the job you had done on Grant's brother, and his wife in Greensboro. It was very clean I was impressed."

"I appreciate the compliments, but cut to the chase."

"A true Santiago, okay then brother. I'ma tell it straight. I'm in a turf war with a rival named Money-B. He is King Charles grandson."

"You mean the King Charles. The biggest king pin in the South, that old man is a legend. He's untouchable." Justice stated.

"I know damn well who he is, but he's not the problem now. I'm dying, I will be long dead, and in the ground before this war between me, and Money-B is over. I refuse to die knowing that Money-B still lives to take over the Santiago turfs. As it stands now I am unable to physically kill him. Because of my condition I am naming you as my successor. Upon my death you will have control of all my businesses, accounts, and drug turfs and connects that reaches from the states to Japan. You will be a very rich man Justice."

"What's the catch?" Justice asked.

"The catch is you have to earn your seat just as I did. It's the Santiago way."

"What do I have to do?"

"You have to kill Money-B, and bury me when I'm gone."

"What about King Charles?"

"If the King interferes grandma will take care of him they have a deep history together."

"Grandma."

"Yes grandma. Have you not been listening to anything I've said?"

"I have but I'm not clear where grandma fits in all this."

"Grandma is the reason you're here, grandma put me in this position."

"So you're telling me my grandma is a Queen pin?"

"That's exactly what I am telling you. Our grandfather Raymond Santiago died from a hit by King Charles. Vidah Santiago our grandmother took over after she buried her husband, then she killed all of King Charles generals. When she finally got to King Charles for some reason she let him live. Nobody knows for sure why she did it. When our mother came of age she took over and our grandmother retired. Chin told me our mother killed her aunt which was our grandmother's sister."

"Who is Chin?" Justice asked.

"Chin is the man that raised me. He was my father's best friend. We called him China man he was Chinese. He died a couple years ago."

"This is deep. I can't believe grandma never told me any of

this."

"It wasn't time I guess. I don't know what to tell you about that."

"At the end of the day Im'a Santiago, and whatever needs to be done Im'a do it."

"That's good to hear Justice. Here is all the information, I have on Money-B." Kanden replied as he reached inside his desk and pulled out a file and handed it to Justice, who briefly flipped thru the file and spotted a picture of Money-B standing between two women. He took a mental note to start there.

"I will also need your signature on these papers here." Kanden said, as he pulled out another file.

"This is my will. Your signature confirms that you have been told of my request after my death." Kanden said as he passed a pen to Justice.

"I get all this for just a simple murder?"

"This won't be simple. If it was it would already have been done."

"Murder has always been simple for me and my Stunna Boys."

"We'll see then, and please don't tell grandma what I told you. She doesn't like opening old wounds."

"Your secret is safe. I'll handle this in a few weeks. I'll let you know when it's done." Justice replied standing up from his chair. Kanden tried to stand also but Justice stopped him, and walked over and gave him a hug.

"Blood of my blood. Flesh of my flesh. Santiago's for life." Justice whispered to Kanden.

Kanden smiled. "For life brother." He replied as he watched Justice walk out of his office.

Chapter 5

Gifts

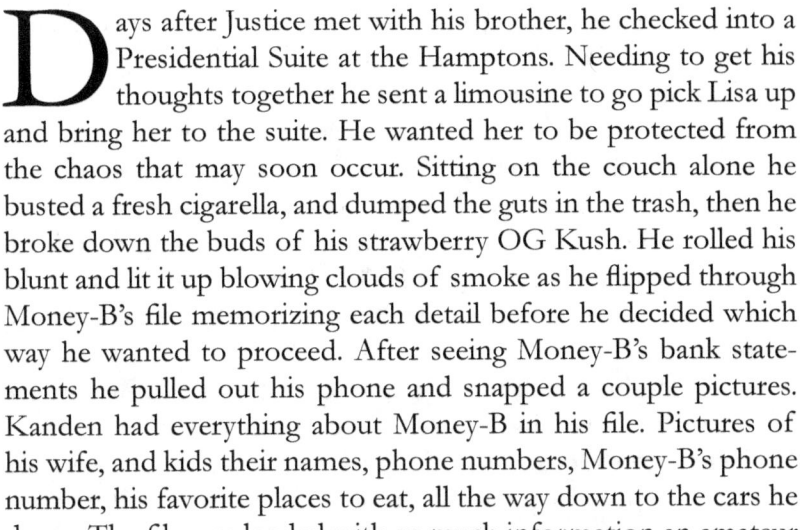

Days after Justice met with his brother, he checked into a Presidential Suite at the Hamptons. Needing to get his thoughts together he sent a limousine to go pick Lisa up and bring her to the suite. He wanted her to be protected from the chaos that may soon occur. Sitting on the couch alone he busted a fresh cigarella, and dumped the guts in the trash, then he broke down the buds of his strawberry OG Kush. He rolled his blunt and lit it up blowing clouds of smoke as he flipped through Money-B's file memorizing each detail before he decided which way he wanted to proceed. After seeing Money-B's bank statements he pulled out his phone and snapped a couple pictures. Kanden had everything about Money-B in his file. Pictures of his wife, and kids their names, phone numbers, Money-B's phone number, his favorite places to eat, all the way down to the cars he drove. The file was loaded with so much information an amateur could knock this guy off. Seeing all this information he called his homeboy Hawk who was a pure computer genius. Hawk picked up on the third ring.

"Hello." Hawk answered.

"What's good homie?"

"Justice."

"Yeah."

"I haven't heard from you in a minute. How are you doing man?" Hawk asked.

"Shit has been kinda hectic, but I'm good tho." Justice replied.

"That's good to know, but what's up tho?"

"I'm calling bearing gifts."

"What you need homie?" Hawk asked wanting to know what's up.

"You have anything that can steal information from a person's computer?" Justice asked.

"Yeah, I think I may have something for you. It's similar to what you're asking for, but I can tweak it a little to meet your demands I'm sure."

"How soon and how much is it going to hit me for."

"Shit give me a couple hours. Since we're cool just give me five bands, and we'll call it square." Hawk answered.

"Aite hit me back when everything's ready."

"I got cha." Hawk replied before ending the call.

Justice hung up shaking his head and laughing to himself at how crazy his homie was. He knew Hawk was crazy when he first met the white boy with nappy dreads, but when he found out Hawk had gotten kicked out of ITT Tech for hacking into the schools security server. He knew then that he had to have Hawk on his team.

Checking his watch it was a quarter to 9 in the morning. He knew it would take Lisa a while before she arrived at the hotel, so he decided to shoot through the Trey-four to scope out some of Money-B's spots to get a full visual layout of who and what he was dealing with.

Grabbing his keys he headed out the door, and hopped in his rented charger, and headed down Highway 103 that connects into Business 52. He gets off Peter Creek Parkway exit moments later he turned onto west Sprague Street. On his GPS Justice finds Devonshire Road. After locating one of Money-B's houses, a two story modular home. Justice parks close to the house, and snaps a few photos from different angles. When he finished he pulled off and headed over to east Martin Luther King Boulevard where he took pictures of Money-B's car dealership, barbershop, and clothing store. He was trying to figure out the best strategic spot to attack from. Being that all of Money-B's businesses were closer together it would be difficult for what he was planning. Remembering what he had seen in Money-B's file. He remembered Money-B daughter Amanda was enrolled at Forsyth Tech. Doting his I's, and crossing his T's Justice pulled off and headed that way. Once on the campus Justice parked his car and got out and began to walk through the campus. Feeling out of place he walked into one of the campus gift shops and bought a book bag and a few books, a F.T.I. tee shirt, cap, and a campus map. Blending in with the rest of the students. He followed the direction on the campus as he located each class that Money-B daughter was enrolled in snapping pictures along the way.

It was now 1:30pm and classes were letting out. Justice headed toward Amanda's biology class. The influx of students rushing to their next class made it easy for him to hide in plain sight. Instantly he spotted his target and moved slowly walking behind her as she entered her classroom. He sat in class and watched her until class let out. Returning to his car, he remembered that Amanda worked at Planet Fitness on the North Side at night around 9:00pm. He figured that would be the best time to grab her, if he chose that route. Before pulling off he sent all the information he had gathered to Hawk with instruction to create a flash drive to store all of the photos in. He then placed a call to Amir to let him know what his course of action would be. He wanted to strike hard causing fear, and panic. He also wanted to hit Money-B's pockets at the same time. With everything done Justice pulled off headed back to his hotel to meet Lisa.

Amir, Red Bull, and Harlem World were kicking it on the Dirt Road, when Amir received a call from Justice. A couple days back Justice had spoken to him about meeting with his brother. Justice was full of emotions as he vented to him about what he had to do. The murder was nothing that hasn't been done before. It was the fact that Justice had found out he had a brother, and in the same sentence found out that he was dying of cancer. Amir was Justice's brother not by blood, but by loyalty, and he promised that he would always be there for him to the very end no matter how many lives they had to take, he would be there, and so would the rest of the Stunna Boys.

"Yo what the Bro talking bout?" Harlem World asked.

"Not much you already know how Justice is, he's headed back to Martinsville now. He has something he's putting together. We might have to put in some work soon." Amir answered.

"You just let me know Akhi, my gun stay ready." Harlem World replied.

"I already know." Amir said stating facts.

"Yo Bull you ready." Harlem asked.

"You know what's up wit me. If it makes money it makes sense."

They all laughed, as they continued to pass the blunt around the cipher.

As soon as Justice pulled in the parking lot of his hotel, where he had his presidential suite. His phone began to ring. He looked at the caller I.D. and saw that it was Hawk.

"Yo what's up Bro?" Justice answered.

"I got what you asked for." Hawk said.

"Bet." Justice stated. "Peep it tho. I need a phone tap on those numbers I sent you. I need it on an alternate source on a forty-eight hour loop."

"That'll be a cake walk. I'll have everything on a separate device. How soon do you want it?" Hawk asked.

"Shit preferably today if possible." Justice stated urgently.

"You're pushing it bro. I'll work as fast as I can it maybe tomorrow tho putting this type of stuff together takes time."

"That's fine I have to meet up with Lisa in a few anyways."

"You still with that girl?" Hawk asked.

"Yeah that's my ride or die."

"You got a good one. She's always been bad."

"Watch your mouth now."

"My bad bruh, no harm no foul. I'm just letting you know you got a good one on your side."

"It's all good, I'll hit you up tomorrow."

"Tomorrow it is peace." Hawk said as he hung the phone up.

Justice hung up and got out of his car taking the elevator up to his suite. When he got inside he undressed and took a shower. He wanted to be ready before Lisa arrived which would be shortly. Once he got dressed in his Vamp life outfit. He thought he was running late so he called down to the reception desk to see if Lisa had arrive yet to his satisfaction she had not. Glad that he wasn't running late, and he could take his time, he went to the bathroom and put on a dab of cologne. Sure of himself after taking a double take in the mirror, he headed out and took the private elevator downstairs to meet his queen. When he got downstairs he realized he was right on time. The limo had just pulled up. A smile spread across his face as he watched his queen step out of the limo. Lisa's dress game was on point. She was rocking a red Vera Wang dress that looked like it had been airbrushed on her skin, she wore a pair of red and black six inch heels that showed off her perfectly pedicured toes that were also painted red to match her dress. He couldn't ask for a better queen; he thought to himself, as he straightened himself up, and walked towards his lady.

"Hey baby you look beautiful. I love the dress and the heels." Justice said, as he hugged Lisa, and lightly kissed her.

"Thank you, I hope I haven't overdressed. When you sent a limo to pick me up with a backseat full of roses I didn't know what to expect. I figured you had something special planned." Lisa replied.

"Nonsense, you look lovely. Come on let's get in. I'm starving." Justice said helping Lisa back inside the limo. The driver pulled off heading to their destination.

"How was the ride?"

"It was aite." Lisa answered playfully.

"Really, baby next time it will be a hooptee with no heat or stereo." Justice shot back.

"I'm just playing baby the ride was perfect thank you for my roses."

"Your welcome, I'll always give you the best as long as you're mine." Justice replied humbly.

After a thirty minute drive they were finally pulling up to the five star restaurant Justice had picked out for this special occasion. He helped her out of the limo and the both walked inside.

"Mr. Santiago your table is ready sir." The maître-d stated as she lead the beautiful couple to the V.I.P. table Justice had requested.

Sitting down, without hesitation Justice reached inside his pocket and pulled out his wallet and gave the maître-d a fifty dollar tip.

"Thank you sir, your menus are on the way. Will you and the lovely lady be having champagne tonight?" The maître-d asked.

"Yes I'll let the lady order, since this is her night." Justice answered nodding his head in Lisa's direction.

"How about some white, if you have it." Lisa requested.

"Yes right away." The maître-d replied as he hurried away leaving the two of them alone.

"Oh my God baby you put me on the spot. I didn't know

what to order." Lisa admitted honestly.

"Don't worry it wasn't a life or death situation. You'll have plenty of time to practice."

"Oh really, what you got going on Justice?"

"Nothing I just want to treat you good is all."

"You already treat me good."

"I just want the best for you is all. Let's just enjoy tonight okay."

"Okay."

After the waitress came back with the menus they both ordered their food, and ate, and laughed enjoying each other company. When they finally returned to the hotel they couldn't keep their hands off each.

"I love you so much." Justice whispered as he laid Lisa gently down on the king sized bed.

"I know you do, I love you too."

The rest of the night they explored each other's limits as they forgot the world around them from being lost in each other's arms.

The next day Justice woke up early in the morning. When he got up, he grabbed a half of a blunt out of the ashtray, and lit it up, as he sat up on the bed, and watched as Lisa slept. He loved her so much even tho she was white. She was the only woman he wanted. He hated the way some people looked at them, when they were out in public. It was as if they hated to see a black man with a white woman. The truth was they didn't care what people thought of them as long as the love was there that's all that ever mattered to Justice and to him the love was always there. When Justice finished smoking the half of blunt he dumped the roach in the ashtray, then he leaned over, and kissed Lisa on her forehead, before he got up and took a shower. When he finished he got dressed, and brushed his teeth. Justice's phone began to vibrate he picked it up, and looked at the caller I.D. and seen that it was Hawk, so he answered.

"What up bruh?"

"What's good?"

"You ready for me?"

"Yeah, meet me in Durham off the Pizza Hut exit, you remember the old spot?"

"Yeah I remember, I'll be there. I'm driving a blue Charger."

"Pull around the back."

"I got cha Hawk. I'll see you in about a hour."

When Justice got off the phone he threw on a shirt and walked over to the bed, and woke Lisa up.

"What is it baby?" Lisa asked.

"I gotta make a run real quick. I'll be back in a few."

"Where are you going, come back to bed with me baby." Lisa said in a whispered sleepy voice.

"I can't baby I gotta meet somebody, and pick something up. You can order whatever you want room service will bring it up. I left a stack on the table just in case you need to do something." Justice replied.

"When will you be back?"

"It should only take a couple of hours then I'm all yours."

"Okay I'll be here waiting on you."

"Thanks love." Justice replied then he tongue kissed Lisa, grabbed his keys, and shot out the door. When he pulled up at the Pizza Hut in Durham, Hawk was already parked around back waiting for him in his Dodge Journey. Justice pulled up right beside him and got out the car.

"What up Hawk, long time no see."

"I know right." Hawk replied as he dapped Justice up.

"Aite, what you got for me?"

Hawk walked to the back of his Dodge Journey, and had lifted the back door, and pulled out a small device.

"Okay now this here is my latest creation. It's called the account eraser, all you have to do is load his account numbers and debit card number into this device, then punch in the account numbers to where you want the money to be transferred, then bingo it's gone. Just that easy. This second device here is for the wire taps that you asked for. I created a app and logged the numbers you requested in. The taps are automatically linked."

"Is it working now?" Justice asked.

"Yes, let me show you." Hawk answered as he opened the app, and clicked on one of the loaded numbers. He then pulled out a set of headphones from his pocket, and plugged them into the phone. Immediately the current conversation was uploaded he then passed the headphones to Justice.

"Just listen."

Justice grabbed the small headsets, and placed them in his ears. He heard a female voice come over the airwaves. He listened for a second then smiled as he realized whose voice he was hearing. It was Money-B's daughter. Justice then cut the phone off.

"I could kiss you right about now. Question, can I punch any number in this app?" Justice.

"No, the tap will only work on the numbers that I already uploaded, there is also a tracker installed. A red dot will come up on any location where those phone are at. All you have to do is press the located button on the app."

"Damn boy, you a fool wit it this makes what I have to do a whole lot easier."

"Glad you are satisfied, now as we all say show me the money." Hawk said.

"That's not a problem my man." Justice said as he reached in his pocket, and pulled out eight bands, he thought about giving Hawk the five bands that he asked for, but said fuck it and handed him the whole bank roll.

"Damn homie how much is this? I only asked for five."

"It's eight racks your five plus three more consider it a tip bruh."

"Good look fam, if you need me again it's on the house. It makes me happy when my friends appreciate my work."

"Thanks tho bro." Justice replied dapping Hawk up.

"No problem just be careful, and stay in touch." Hawk replied, then released from their embrace and got in his car and pulled off. Justice did the same, turning up his sound system ready to put his plan together.

Atlanta G.A.

Money-B sat with his grandfather King Charles as he underwent his regular dialysis treatment. King Charles was the biggest king pin in the south. If he wanted you gone, all he had to do was snap his fingers, and it would be a reality. Money-B looked up to his grandfather, he was the only man that could humble him. He missed his long talks and chess matches with him and the parties on his yacht. But since his kidneys went bad he stayed in his mansion most of the time surrounded by his soldiers. Money-B came to see him twice a week.

All he ever talked about was eliminating the Santiago family. But what Money-B didn't understand was why his grandfather would never send his hit team to take Kanden out. He had the power to do so, but for some reason he never lifted a finger. Money-B knew better than to questions his grandfather, even tho he started this war with Kanden because it is what he asked. When Money-B needed direction the only answer King Charles would say was that in order to be king he had to win this war leave no Santiago alive King Charles always said. Money-B never knew where all this hatred came from the only thing that mattered was doing what his grandfather asked. If he wanted the Santiago's dead he would kill them all.

"Grandfather, are you alright today?" Money-B asked.

"I'm fine grandson, I see you haven't forgotten a old man." King Charles replied.

"I would never forget you grandpa."

"I know, tell me how is my great granddaughter?"

"She is well, she's staying up on her studies. I think in the end she will do well for the family. She goes to school, and work. She likes to stay busy."

"That is good to hear. I want you to keep her safe grandson. She is my little princess. There is no rules in war, only that you win by any means necessary, protect your family keep them guarded."

"Kanden would never lift a finger at my family."

"What did I tell you stupid boy?" King Charles replied, as he slapped Money-B across the face making him fall from his chair. King Charles's general stepped forward after seeing King Charles become angry he reached in his coat for his pistol ready to end Money-B's life.

"Hold Ra'mon, I'm okay put that gun away my grandson is just a stupid boy, but yet and still this stupid boy is my blood. Show him to the door."

"But grandpa." Money-B said.

"Silence, it is time for you to go."

Ra'mon walked over to help Money-B off the floor.

"Get your hands off me. I know my way out." Money-B said, brushing Ra'mon's hands away from him, gathering his thoughts he stood up and walked out. On the way to the airport to catch the earliest flight back to the Carolina's, Money-B pulled out his phone and called Rondo.

'Ring', 'Ring'.

"What up boss?" Rondo answered.

"Have one of your soldiers swing thru Kanden's shopping plaza. Take the twins out, matter of fact fuck it send Danger. I want this shit done right."

"I'm on it." Rondo replied.

"Rondo."

"Yeah."

"I want it messy. I want that sick muthafucka to feel this one worse than the last."

"Don't worry. I'll have it taken care of."

"I never do." Money-B said and hug the phone up, and walked inside the airport to board his flight.

Chapter 6

Hammer Time

12:00pm Wednesday Night

Danger sped his Nova down Church Street, his phone vibrated in his lap. He picked it up and saw that it was a text from Money-B's general letting him know who his next two victims were. Diamond Twinz was all the text said. Danger smiled to himself already knowing who they were and exactly where to find them. The Diamond Twinz were well known in Burlington, they loved showing off always riding in twin old schools with big motors, and big rims they stayed in the strip club making it rain on all the girls. They were the life of every party, certified dope boys. Danger made a right at the light, and mashed on the gas pedal taking his Nova to 65 mph. He was headed straight to the interstate knowing that the Diamond Twinz would be at Club Starlight as they were every night after 12:00pm.

Forty minutes later Danger was pulling into the parking lot of Club Starlight bringing his Nova to a slow creep, and scanning the parking lot. Almost instantly Danger spotted Marco and Lex's twin all cherry red 1977 Corvettes sitting on 24's. Checking his .357's Danger pulled to the back of the club, and parked his Nova. He got out slowly making sure his hammers were well concealed. He thought about hiding under one of the twin's Corvettes, but knew it would be hours before they came out. Deciding against the idea. Danger walked to the front entrance. When one of the bouncers came to pat him down he handed him three hundred dollar bills. The bouncer already knew what it was. After taking Danger's money he let him right through, and even gave him a V.I.P. pass. Danger dapped the bouncer up, and kept it moving inside. When Danger walked inside the club lights were flashing everywhere it was two light skinned girls on stage twerking, and spreading their ass cheeks. Two dark skinned guys were standing in front of the stage throwing wads of money. Danger wanted to take his time, so he walked to the bar.

"What will you be having?" The naked bartender asked.

"Let me get a shot of patron."

"Patron it is coming right up."

Danger watched as the naked bartender walked away. If he wasn't there on business he would definitely hit that he thought to himself. The bartender came back, and poured his shot. He picked up the glass, and threw it back.

"Hit me again." Danger said asking for another shot. The naked bartender pours another shot. Danger threw that one back also.

"Let me get a Bud light."

"Coming up." The bartender stuck her hand in the refrigerator, and pulled out a cold beer and popped the top for him.

"Let me get another shot, and what's your name?"

"My name is Shelly." The bartender said as she poured Danger's third shot.

"It's nice to meet you Shelly. Here, this is for you it's enough for the drinks and a tip." Danger replied as he handed her a hundred dollar bill, and grabbed his drinks.

"Uh what are you doing later? I'm free after work."

Danger smiled. "Another time ma." Danger said, as he walked off making his way over to the section where Marco and Lex were at. Danger went and took a table at the back where he could take notice of his surroundings. When he finished his drinks he was feeling a lil tipsy, so he sat, and gathered himself together. When he lifted his head he saw that Marco and Lex were walking to the back with two strippers. He figured now was a good time. Pulling his .357 from under his coat Danger got up from the table, and followed Marco, and Lex. Once in the back of the club there were six rooms that the girls use to entertain customers. Danger didn't know what room Marco and Lex went in or if they were even in the same room or different rooms. Creeping slowly, *Damn why did I take those drinks* Danger thought to himself, as he pressed on. When he got to the first room he peeked through the curtain neither of the twins were inside, so he moved onto the next which was also empty. When he got to the third room he peeked in the same as he did the other two. Marco was sitting on the couch with his pants around his ankles getting his dick sucked by one of the light skinned girls that was dancing on stage when he walked in the club. Danger crept inside his .357 leading the way. The girl on her knees seen him first, and screamed by the time Marco looked up it was too late Danger shot him two times in the chest. The thunder clap of Danger's hammer caused panic in the back of the club. When Danger walked out the room the first person he saw was Lex. Before Danger could raise his .357 Lex fired 3 shots from his Glock in Danger's direction. Danger ducked for cover as he returned fire blindly, crouched on the floor behind a small wall. Danger slung open the chamber to his .357, and dumped the empty shells in his hand, as he stuck them in his pocket he slipped in his auto reloader, and slung the chamber back in place. Danger looked around the wall and saw Lex take off running, he gave chase running right behind Lex pushing strippers, and Johns out the way. Lex shot thru the exit door, and fired two more rounds in Danger's direction. Danger ducked and fired back hitting Lex in his left knee cap. Lex instantly fell to the ground dropping his gun as he hit the pavement. Lex tried to stand but couldn't bring himself back to his feet. Lex's Corvette was two cars up his Dreko was behind his passenger seat he began to drag himself praying that he would be able to reach his car before it was too late. Danger seeing that Lex was hit he began to walk slowly like a predator stalking it's prey. When Danger walked around the parked cars he saw Lex's feet dangling on the ground with half of his body inside his Corvette. Danger lifted his .357, and fired a round that hit Lex square in the hip. The impact caused Lex to slide out of his car his head hitting the concrete. His Dreko was still in sight Lex willed his body to move, but neither of his limbs listened. Lex closed his eyes knowing that death was close. Danger stood over Lex with his gun pointed at his forehead. "Damien." Lex whispered right before Danger pulled the trigger ending Lex's life.

"Sorry kid this was just business." Danger mumbled to himself then he took off in a light jog got inside his Nova, and pulled off like nothing had just happened.

Once Danger hit the interstate he pulled out his phone and texted Rondo one word. "Done." Then he hit the send button.

Thursday 8:00am

Hello I'm Diana James, this is Channel 8 News good morning. Last night there was a shootout in Greensboro at Starlight strip club two males were found dead, Marcus Simmons and Luther Simmons both 28 years old they both suffered multiple gunshot wounds and died on the scene there are no suspects at this time. Anyone with information please call 1-800-Crimestoppers.

Kanden sat in his living room furious as he drunk his cup of coffee, and watched the 8:00 o'clock news. Seeing the Diamond Twinz faces pop up on the news touched him in ways he couldn't begin to explain. He had raised those boys, he had put them on he showed them the game they had died because of his beef, Rio had died also. Kanden sat his coffee down, and banged his fist on the table cursing himself because of his weakness. If it wasn't for his cancer, he would have been ended this war. Kanden picked up his phone and dialed one of his lieutenant's numbers.

'Ring, Ring'.

"You seen the news?" Kanden asked.

"Yeah, I just finished watching it." Gunz replied.

"Send a message to that fuck boy. Go to his turf and air it out."

"Say no more I'm on it." Gunz replied just before Kanden hung up.

After Kanden hung the phone up he laid his head back on the couch. Hoping Justice was the man that Vidah Santiago thought her grandson was. He was the key to winning and he prayed his brother would come thru for the family before his cancer took him then it would be all over, and the generation of the Santiago line would be erased by his death.

Mid-afternoon

Justice, Amir, Harlem World, and Red Bull all sat at Amir's house on the Dirt Road, and listened as Justice ran his game plan down to his Stunna Boys.

"Yo ya'll are my brothers, I've already spoken to Amir about me finding out that I have a brother and that he is dying of cancer. His name is Kanden, ya'll might know him as Kandyman."

"You talking about the dude that got all the work, and all the businesses in Burlington, Raleigh, and Durham." Red Bull replied.

"Yeah that's him."

"Kandyman, Kandyman I've been hearing his name ringing out in Greensboro they say he doing big numbers, but he suppose to be sick or something." Harlem World stated.

"As I've already said he has cancer he's dying and wants to hand his operation over to me."

"Let's get this money then." Amir interrupted.

"Hold my friend there is a condition that has to be met first."

"What's the condition?" Harlem World asked.

"I'm trying to tell ya'll if ya'll quit fucking interrupting me." Justice spat.

"Anyway what I was saying the condition is that I have to kill Money-B, and then bury him after he dies of his cancer. I know this sounds easy but for some reason or another my brother can't even kill this guy. I have a file with everything about Money-B that was given to me." Justice said as he pulled the file out, and placed it on the table, and he watches as Harlem World was the first to grab it.

"I have a plan."

"What do you have in mind?" Amir asked.

"I did a little recon-ing on my own, and I had Hawk create me a device that taps their phones. Money-B has a daughter name Amanda, she goes to school in Winston at Forsyth Tech and she works at Planet Fitness at night. I figure we can kidnap her, and force Money-B out, and when he pops his head out that's when we cut it off." Justice explained.

"So we need to put this murder game down. I'm wit cha on that by looking at this file. We can do this if we apply the right amount of pressure." Harlem World said.

"We're a team bro. You ride we all ride. I'm down for whatever homie, you've always had our back when you up we up."

"I can't do this without ya'll." Justice said.

"We got you, how soon you wanta do this? I'm thinking next week, I've been watching his daughter, and it seem Money-B has a little muscle following her around." Justice answered Red Bull.

"Well we'll lay their asses down too." Harlem World replied.

"Say no more then fellas. I'm bout to bounce. I promised Lisa I would be home tonight she cooking shrimp Alfredo ya'll know how she is about cooking. I say Monday we execute Plan A."

"Monday sounds good to us." Amir replied.

Justice then stood up, and dapped all his bros up and walked out.

Chapter 7

Hell is Hot

Saturday 11:15pm

Gunz, and six of his soldiers suited up armed with AR-15's, and AK's, Kanden wanted a message sent, and he had promised his boss that he would get the job done. *It's time for some action.* Gunz thought to himself hopping into the passenger seat of the black Tahoe. The Diamond Twinz were his bros Money-B will pay for what they did to them.

"Ya'll load up." Gunz hollered as he watched the rest of his squad get into the SUV behind his. They pulled off headed to High Point.

Once they got to High Point everyone inside the SUV's were locked, and ready. They checked, and re-checked their weapons this was not a time for mistakes or misfires. As soon as they entered the hood Clara Cox which was owned by Money-B, both

SUV's split up, Gunz head over to Ashboro Street the other SUV swerved over to Randolph St. When Gunz pulled on Ashboro there were a bunch of people running back, and forth to cars making sales. Gunz had his driver park, and they watched as a group of guys sat on the porch of a white house, and drunk beers, and smoked blunts. Looking through a set of binoculars Gunz thought for a second that he seen Rondo amongst the crowd. It was no time to think he had to hit before the second team hit a few streets over. Gunz spoke in his walkie talkie.

"Are you in position?" Gunz.

"Yeah we're posted it's at least ten people out here."

"Move in, take as many out as you can, over."

"Copy bro, we're moving in now."

Gunz dropped his walkie talkie, and pulled up his AR. "Let's move, pull up in front of that white house and stop as soon as you do hang your AK out that window." Gunz said then his soldier pulled off. Gunz rolled the window down and sat on the passenger door with his body hanging outside and his AR-15 aimed over the roof.

As soon as the SUV was in front of the white house Gunz opened fire.

Thratt, Thratt, Thrattt.

It was clear pandemonium. Bodies dropped all over the place. Gunz driver slammed the SUV in park hanging his AK out the driver side window. He squeezed the trigger showing no mercy, more bodies fell as they both emptied their clips. "Let's go." Gunz yelled to his driver pulling his AK back inside the SUV. He slammed the Tahoe in drive, and hit the gas taking the SUV to 40 mph they could still hear gun fire coming from the street over. "Link up with the other team." Gunz said as he reloaded his AR-15. Turning down Randolph Street Gunz shot everything moving. When they linked up with the second Tahoe, Gunz got on his walkie talkie again, "let's head out." When both SUV's pulled back on the main street a patrol car shot out the parking lot at the Kon's mini mart. "Shit." Gunz yelled as the cop car tried to block the road. "Ram that fucking pig." Gunz yelled.

His soldier doing as he was told rammed the side of the police cruiser. Gunz held his AR-15 out the window, and shot down inside the police cruiser. 'Thratt.' 'Thratt.' Instantly killing the cop inside. The second SUV pulled around the front of Gunz and the back door shot open. Gunz and his driver jumped out of there wrecked SUV, and jumped in the back of the other SUV. The driver sped off heading to the interstate. Once they were safely on Highway 85 Gunz calmed down. "Good job guys Kanden will be proud, and give you all raises." Gunz said to his soldiers as he pulled out his phone, and called Kanden.

'Ring.'

"Yo." Kanden picked on the first ring waiting for Gunz call, drinking a shot of cognac.

"Clara Cox has been taken care of." Was all Gunz said.

Kanden didn't say a word he remained silent then hung his phone up, and lit his cigar smiling to himself.

Sunday morning 8:00 am

Hi I'm Sandra Johnson reporting from channel 5 news with your 8:00 update. Last night was a sad day in High Point 8 people were killed seven more were injured in a shootout in the neighborhood of Clara Cox. One police officer was murdered as he tried to stop the suspects from fleeing. The officer's dash cam caught a brief video of the suspects, no one has been identified at this time anyone with information please call 1-800-crimes-toppers.

Money-B threw an ashtray at his 60 inch television cracking the screen. "Muthafuckas." Money-B screamed. "Get the fuck up and get out." Money-B screamed at the two women that lay naked on his couch. He watched them both as they hurried to put their clothes on, and ran out the door. When they were gone Money-B grabbed his cellphone off the table, and dialed Rondo's number.

'Ring' 'Ring' 'Ring'.

"Hello." Rondo answered.

"Hello my ass, what the fuck happened down there last night, why am I seeing dead bodies in my neighborhood?" Money-B hollered.

"Boss, they just pulled in, and started shooting. We were caught off guard. We didn't know what was happening until it was too late."

"You were there?"

"Yeah."

"I'm at the house in Charlotte get your ass up here now." Money-B screamed in the phone and then hung up.

8:30 am High Point Police department

The baldheaded bearded man wearing a cowboy hat and a pair of snake skin cowboy books with a .357 hanging from his shoulder holster walked inside the police department and stopped at the reception desk, then reached down to his waist grabbed his badge and sat it on the desk.

"My name is Jacobe Slade Special agent with the F.B.I. I'm here to see police Chief Turner."

The officer running the reception desk examined the badge on his desk then picked it up and handed it back to the agent, then he got on the phone and called Chief Turner.

'Ring' 'Ring'.

"Hello Chief Turner speaking."

"Sir, there's a F.B.I. agent by the name of Jacobe Slade here to see you sir." The reception officer said.

"Send him up right away Scott."

"Yes sir he's on the way." Officer Scott replied and then hung up.

"Take the elevator second floor third door on the right." Officer Scott said to the agent.

Agent Slade tipped his hat, and thanked the officer, then he walked to the elevator. When he got off he walked into the Captains office.

"Hello Captain."

"How are you? Have a seat Agent Slade."

Agent Slade sat down.

"So what brings the famous cowboy down to North Carolina let alone High Point?"

"The murders that happened in Clara Cox." Agent Slade replied.

"Those murders were from a drive by shooting between the gangs here in High Point. Detective Chambers is investigating." Captain Turner said.

"I think different. I believe the murders in Greensboro, the two twins, the murders here in High Point. The murders of Rio AKA Remy Davis and his wife Alicia Davis. I strongly believe all of these murder are connected."

"And why would you believe that?" Chief Turner asked.

"For starts Remy Davis. I know for sure is connected to the Santiago family. These murders that happened in your city were Santiago style hits. I believe that the family war from 15 years ago is back. It's not fact call it a hunch Chief."

"I pray this is not what you think it is. Those years were sad years, we were all happy when you took Danielle Santiago down."

"I was lucky Chief Turner that her husband worked with me to stop her. I'm going to go visit him when I leave here." Agent Slade replied.

"I think that will be a good idea, so we can get a real feel of what we're dealing with here."

"So I have your full cooperation, and the cooperation of this department." Agent Slade asked.

"Our objectives are the same to catch these guys, and lock them away. All I ask is that we put this cop killer in the ground. I want to bring his family peace. I don't want them bothered by appeals and M.A.R.'s trials, I don't want them to have to relive these moments again. You are the famous cowboy that took down the Santiago Queen. You will always have the help of this department as long as I am Chief."

"I will do the best I can Chief Turner, but I hope this is not what I think it is." Agent Slade replied as he got up and shook Chief Turner's hand. He put his cowboy hat back on his head, and walked out of his office. When Agent Slade finally walked out of the High Point Police Department he took a deep breath before opening the door to his 2018 F-350. When he got inside he put his key in the ignition then pulled a picture from his pocket of Danielle Santiago and sat it on the dash then he pulled off. *I'm sorry Danielle. I miss you so much.* Agent Slade thought to himself as he pulled off heading to Butner Federal Institution.

After an hour drive from High Point to Durham Agent Slade pulled into the parking lot of Butner. He got out and checked his firearm in a safety box, and put the box key inside his pocket before going inside the prison. When he was inside Butner he checked in with the front office, and produced his badge.

"I'm here to see Christopher Perry." Agent Slade said.

"Alright I'll have him brought up please wait in the visitation room Agent Slade." The correctional officer receptionist replied.

"Thank you ma'am." Agent Slade said as he tipped his hat, and walked to the Marshal Visitation Room. When he walked inside the room was cold, as always, he hated that he had left his coat inside his truck forgetting how it felt inside the V.I. rooms. He pulled a chair up and sat at the table and waited. After waiting for 20 minutes Christopher Perry finally walked in. Christopher had a surprised look on his face when he saw Agent Slade. After sitting down at the V.I. table they finally spoke.

"What the fuck are you doing here Slade?" Christopher asked.
"Agent Slade to you Chris."
"You must be trying to get me killed. It's bad enough you a affair with my wife. Instead of killing you. I let you live and helped you."
"You'll get no thanks from me. If that's what you're asking for."
"I wouldn't dare ask you for shit. I just want to know why you are here."
"There has been two bodies dropped in Burlington, Remy Davis AKA Rio, his wife was murdered also. I know that he works for the Santiago family. Two more bodies dropped in Greensboro and eight more in High Point Saturday."
"So what Slade. But what does that have to do with me?"
"I believe the families are warring again, fighting for control over turf. If so I need your help to help me stop it."
"I helped you once to bring down my wife because it was the right thing to do. And personally I enjoyed the satisfaction of seeing her face when her lover locked her up, and even more happy when she found out I was behind it. I'm not helping you a second time you're on your own on this one."
"What about your son?"
"My son is not in the game. You already know who's running the Santiago family right?"
"Of course I do tell me about King Charles, have you heard anything in here about him?" Agent Slade asked.
"I'm not a snitch Slade. Don't ask me for information."
"You became a snitch when you turned on your wife, and got her a federal life sentence. I covered it up for you so it wouldn't show in your paperwork that's the only reason you're still alive now. If they knew you were the one responsible for taking down the Santiago Queen your name would become Christi not Christopher and you certainly wouldn't have king pin status in here. It's your choice."
"You're right Slade it is so you do whatever it is you have to

do, but as it stands now. I'm not helping you do shit. C.O. I'm ready, take me back to my unit." Christopher said as he got up from the V.I. table leaving Agent Slade looking stupid as the C.O. came and got him and took him back to his unit. Agent Slade sat back in his chair knowing that this case would be harder to solve than the last one.

By midafternoon Rondo arrived at Money-B's Charlotte mansion. Money-B stood on his balcony as he watched Rondo get out of his BMW, and walk inside. Seeing Rondo come in he walked back inside to meet him. As he walked down his stairs he saw Rondo flirting with one of his maids, grabbing her butt.

"Hands off the help Rondo." Money-B said.

"Boss my bad. I didn't mean any disrespect."

"None taken." Money-B replied then he looked over at his house main. "Wendy would you be so kind as to bring us two drinks of whatever you like as long as you make it strong. Bring them to my office please."

"Yes sir Mr. Santiago." Wendy the house maid replied.

"Come on Rondo let's go to my Office and talk." Money-B said.

"Yes sir lead the way." Rondo replied, then followed Money-B to his office. As soon as they got inside Money-B rapidly turned around and snatched Rondo up slamming his back against the wall.

"You need to get a handle on this situation. If for some reason you can't get the job done. I will bring in people who can." Money-B growled.

"I can handle it Mikal." Rondo replied using Money-B's real name.

Money-B stared Rondo in his eyes as if he were looking down into his soul. Money-B released his grip from around Rondo's neck, straightened his partner's shirt, then turned his back and walked behind his desk and sat down.

"I apologize Rondo. I am under a lot of stress. I will be glad when this war is over."

"We will win. I promise you."

"You better hope so because if we don't. It won't matter that we grew up together. I will see you dead because of your failure, and soon after that I will be dead also at the hands of Kanden or maybe my grandfather's general Ra'mon."

Their conversation was interrupted by a knock on the door.

"Come in Wendy." The door then came open and Wendy the house maid walked inside with their drinks, she then handed Money-B and Rondo both of their drinks. She started to turn, and leave, but was stopped by Money-B.

"Wendy would you be so kind as to set that tray on the table, then I would like for you to remove your clothes."

Wendy walked over to one of the end tables, and sat the tray down, then walked back, and stood in front of Money-B and Rondo. Wendy knew what Money-B wanted she was used to it. She hated his ways but didn't care. The money was good and he paid all of her parent's bills and that was all she cared about.

"Remove your clothes Wendy." Money-B said smiling.

Wendy didn't say a word. She slowly unbuttoned her blouse, and let it fall to the floor then she unzipped her dress, and let it fall to the floor also. Seductively she ran her index finger around her hips inside of her panties pulling them off as she kept her eyes locked on Money-B, as she rubbed the inside of her thighs and around her golden pussy hairs that matched her blond hair. When Wendy stood up she began to rub her breast then she unlaced her bra letting her 34 D's fall free, Wendy stood in front of both men naked as she was when she came into the world.

"Thank you Wendy, now come over here and help me relieve a little stress." Money-B said.

Wendy did not reply. She just walked over to Money-B and spun his chair around and began to unbuckle his belt, and slide his jeans to his ankles, then she got on her knees and pulled out his seven inch erect dick out of the slit in his boxers, and slowly sucked him as she stared in his eyes.

"Come on bruh, you got her sucking your dick while I'm sitting in here." Rondo said as he began to get up.

"Sit the fuck down, and be quiet until she's finished." Money-B hollered.

Rondo did as he was told, and sat back in his seat. For the next ten minutes he listened to Wendy slurp and moaned while she sucked Money-B's dick, then he heard the grunts and knew Money-B was busting off in her mouth.

"Oooh baby that was a big one." Wendy said as wiped her mouth using her hand, then she reached inside Money-B desk drawer and grabbed a rag and wiped Money-B's penis off. When she finished cleaning him she stood up and Money-B pulled his pant up back around his waist.

"Take the rest of the day off." Money-B told Wendy as she seductively walked over and picked her clothes up off the floor. She didn't even bother to put them back on, she just grabbed her shoes and walked out making her ass cheeks shake teasing Rondo.

"That's my bitch. Now keep your fucking hands off her ass or next time. I'll have them cut off. Do I make myself clear?" Money-B spat.

Rondo nodded indicating that he understood.

"Good now tell me exactly what happened at Clara Cox."

Chapter 8

Hood Magic

Justice woke up at 11:30 am with his dick still inside Lisa, they had fell asleep cuddled together in that position. Lisa was still asleep he wanted to wake her, so he lean over, and gently ran his tongue around the inside of her right ear, slowly sliding his dick in and out of her still throbbing wet pussy.

"Hmmm." Lisa moaned taking her left hand she grabbed Justices butt, as he slid in and out of her. Lisa began to roll her hips, as she got more aroused.

"Aaaah baby." She continued, when Justice stuck his finger in her mouth she sucked on it like she was sucking a dick. He then rolled her over flat on her stomach, and spread her legs to gain better access. He made love to her slowly from behind. He braced himself placing his hands on the bed by her head, he continued to dig deeper. Lisa grabbed his arm, and bit down on her pillow that she had been laying on.

"Aaaah Justice." Lisa moaned feeling herself coming.

Knowing his woman like the back of his hand. He stopped pumping and waited while she creamed his dick. When he knew she was finished he lifted her up off the bed, and onto her knees, so he could finish her off doggie style. Gripping her butt cheeks he began to pound her from behind. Lisa screamed and hollered, as he rammed all eight inches in her.

"Aaaah ah aaaah." She screamed. "Fuck me baby."

He continued to pound until he felt himself climax, he jerked and grunted releasing his seed inside her instead of pulling out. Lisa dropped to her stomach Justice dropped down with his dick still inside her stroking her a few more times before he finally pulled. Instead of laying back down he got up naked, dick still swinging. Lisa eye him she loved looking at his naked body. Sometimes she wondered what he saw in her, knowing that he could get any woman he wanted but for some reason or another he always chose her.

"Come here." Lisa said.

Justice walked over to her still naked. "What is it baby?" he asked.

"Nothing I just wanted to do this." Lisa replied gently grabbing his limp dick she stroked it, then kissed the head of his penis right before she put it in her mouth slowly sucking him until he was hard all over again, then she took both of her hands and wrapped them around his butt cheeks pushing him faster towards her mouth. Justice knew exactly what she wanted him to do, so he put both hands on the side of her face, and began to fuck her in the mouth until he found himself cuming all over again.

"Damn baby, where that come from?" Justice asked clearly exhausted.

"Just wanted to show you that I appreciate you."

"You got a hell of a way showing it, you trying to drain me."

"I just wanted to make sure you were satisfied."

"I'm always satisfied with you." Justice replied while he gathered his things to take a shower. When he got out of the shower Lisa was in the bed asleep, so he went ahead and got dressed before he woke her up.

"What is it baby?" Lisa asked in a whispered tone.

"I have to handle some things for my brother. I might be gone for a couple days. I'm not sure yet. I'll call and let you know okay."

"You better make sure you do, and whatever it is you're doing. I want you to be careful. Are you taking Amir and his crazy friend Harlem World with you?" Lisa asked.

"Yeah they'll be with me."

"Okay call me alright."

"I will." Justice replied pulling the covers over his girl. Gathering the rest of his things he left.

Driving his truck, he listened to the sound of Money Bag Yo as he headed to the Dirt Road to meet up with Amir. He needed to make sure that everything was in order. Tonight they would grab Money-B's daughter, and the plan had to be flawless. After the brief drive Justice was pulling down the Dirt Road. When he pulled down in the circle, he saw Amir and Harlem World sitting inside an old Cutlass Supreme. The doors and the trunk were open, Harlem World was smoking a blunt. Seeing Justice pull up he got out of the old Cutlass, and threw his hands up. Justice got out of his truck and walked over to his comrades. When he walked up he notices that Amir was inside of the car hooking up a CD player.

"Bruh, did you buy this old school?" Justice asked Amir after he dapped Harlem World up.

"Yeah, I got her for a steal." Amir replied.

"How much you pay?"

"Man this fool gave that old white man twenty-five hundred dollars for that piece of shit." Harlem World informed.

"Man it's worth it, this is a 1967 Cutlass. When I fix her up you'll be saying something different then." Amir replied.

"Maybe but not right now." Harlem World said.

"That wasn't too much. I like it tho. Gotta put some shoes on her. I know somebody that builds motors to so when you're ready, I'll turn you on." Justice said.

"That's what's up bro. Im'a need that." Amir replied.

"I got cha, but let's get down to business is everything set up for tonight?" Justice asked.

"Yeah everything's good." Amir stated.

"I already stole a van. I got it parked around back." Harlem World said.

"Aite let me take a look." Justice replied, then followed Harlem World around the back of the house.

"Here she is, what you think?"

"A Dodge minivan perfect nobody will expect us to be doing anything driving this." Justice stated, then him and Harlem laughed as they walked back around to the front of the house.

Justice pulled out his phone and called his brother Kanden.

Ring, Ring.

"Yeah." Kanden answered.

"What up bro?"

"Not too much, talk to me."

"I'm making my move tonight. I need a place to handle my business, somewhere not too far, and not to close either."

"Aite look I have a warehouse in Mount Airy nobody ever goes there, so you'll be good. I'll text you the address."

"Cool Im'a holler at you later text the info."

"I'm on it now." Kanden replied hanging up the phone so he could text his brother the address. Five minutes later Justice looked at his phone, and saw the text, then he forwarded the text to Hawk, and also told him to set up a camera with a live feed that could be transmitted to a cell phone. Hawk immediately texted back, letting him know he was on it.

Justice walked over to Amir. "I have a warehouse in Mount Airy where we are going to take Money-B's daughter. I'm bout to head that way now, so I can meet Hawk and set everything up."

"You need me to come with you?"

"No, after everything is set up, Im'a text you the address. I want you and Harlem World to come pick me up, then we'll go execute the grab and bring her back." Justice instructed.

"We'll be here waiting."

"I know it bro. Make sure you bring the AR's just in case we run into trouble. You know they have light security on her."

"Already, no worries from me, and Harlem got you." Amir replied as he dapped Justice up then Justice walked over to Harlem World, and dapped him up. "See ya'll in a few hours."

"Bet it up." Harlem World replied.

Justice walked back to his truck and got inside, and pulled off heading to Mount Airy. It took him a little over an hour to get to Mount Airy from Chapel Hill. When he got to his destination Justice was surprised at how big the warehouse was. To his surprise Hawk was already outside waiting for him in his van. Justice called Kanden back and asked him how to get inside. Kanden gave him the digital code to punch in in order to unlock the doors. After getting what he needed he hung up and got out of his truck and walked over to Hawk.

"What's up playa?" Justice said as Hawk got out.

"Not too much. I have all the equipment we need in the back." Hawk replied as he dapped Justice up.

"Let's get to work then." Justice said as he turned around and walked to the warehouse.

He looked up and found the digital pad, then he punched in the numbers Kanden had given him. The warehouse door locked popped open. Justice pulled the door open, and him, and Hawk walked inside. The place was huge, big enough to fit six transfer truck inside. It had an upstairs that led to a huge office. Seeing this they both walked upstairs and stumbled on an office that was fully furnished.

"We can set everything up in here." Justice said.

"Sounds good to me, let's unload the van. It's going to take me about a hour to hook everything up." Hawk replied.

"Okay, let's get moving then." Justice said, as he walked out of the warehouse office with Hawk following close behind.

It took them both forty-five minutes to unload Hawk's van. He had monitors, and cameras, and tons of wire and camera stands. When everything was unloaded and brought inside Hawk went straight to work. While Hawk worked his magic Justice stepped outside and rolled up a blunt of gas, as he waited patiently. After about an hour Justice's phone began to ring. When he answered it Hawk's face appeared on his screen.

"Can you see me?"

"Yeah."

"Can you hear me clear?"

"Yeah."

"Okay, come in here so I can show you how to work this equipment."

Justice hung his phone up, and walked back up to the warehouse office.

When Justice walked inside the office it looked like he was in a home studio. Hawk had the monitor set up with a camera facing the office desk chair, there was a digital pad sitting on a stand next to the monitor.

"Yo this is some high tech shit." Justice said.

Hawk laughed. "It just looks that way. The system is really simple to work."

"Show me."

"Well all you have to do is hit this button here. It turns on the monitors, and the cameras, then come over here and punch the phone number into this pad. If the person you're calling has a 4G phone your image will automatically pop up it doesn't matter if they have facetime app or not. The system automatically hacks the phone. Okay now that I've showed you. Let me see you do it yourself, so I'll know you got it." Hawk said flipping the switch turning the system off.

Justice did as Hawk asked of him. He punched in Amir's number, and went through all of the steps Hawk had showed him. When Amir answered his face popped up on the monitor.

"Can you see me?"

"Yeah I can see you bruh. But tell me how the fuck am I looking at your face on my phone." Amir asked.

"I take it you can hear me clear."

"Yeah I can hear you bruh. Tell me what the hell is going on?"

"Hawk created this system."

"That white boy is a fool." Amir said.

"Suit up it's time. When I hang up. Im'a text you the address." Justice replied and then hung up.

"This is some bad ass shit." Justice said as he reached in his pocket and pulled out twenty-five hundred dollars and handed it to Hawk.

"Nah Bruh, this one is on the house. The next one I'm charging." Hawk replied.

"I'm fine with that, you do such a good job. I don't mind paying you what you're worth."

"I know bruh that's why I like dealing with you. You always keep it real. I'm bout to get up outta here. I got a hot date tonight." Hawk said dapping Justice up.

"Aite fam thanks. I'll hit you later." Justice replied pulling out his phone he texted Amir.

After Hawk left Justice sat at the old warehouse and waited for his comrades to show up. It took a lil over an hour before Amir was pulling up in the minivan. When Justice's phone rang he didn't answer, he just walked outside and got in the van.

Chapter 9

What's Yours is Mine

Pulling up into the Planet Fitness parking lot Justice checked the time they were twenty minutes early it was eight-forty. Knowing that Money-B's daughter was precise when it came to being on time.

"Harlem do you see those two guys parked over there in the BMW, they are the ones running security on Amanda. I need for you to take them out before we can grab the girl." Justice said.

"No problem I can handle that." Harlem World said, then reached in his bag, and pulled out his Glock then pulled his ski-mask down over his face. "Don't do nothing until I come back." Harlem World said as he hopped out the back of the van.

"You got ten minutes." Justice replied.

"I'll only need five." Harlem World shot back then took off into a light jog.

When Harlem World got close to the BMW he rolled his ski

mask up, and tucked his Glock. He grabbed a beer bottle off the ground that someone had left in the parking lot. Then he put on his Oscar performance, he started walking like he was drunk. When he got to the BMW he staggered, and fell on the hood, both guys got out of the BMW as they watched a drunk man pass out on the hood of their car.

"Yo what the fuck are you doing? Get your drunk ass off my car." Money-B's goon said.

Then both goons tried to lift Harlem off the hood of the car. After getting both men close Harlem World went into instant action, grabbing both men by the neck Harlem pushed them backwards then kicked the one on the left in the chest dropping him to the ground at the same time, he pulled his Glock from his waist, and pistol whipped the other goon instantly knocking him out. Before the other goon could pull his weapon Harlem World had his Glock pointed at him.

"Don't think about it mutha fucka slowly toss that gun on the ground." Harlem World said.

The goon didn't say a word. He didn't wanta die, so he slowly complied tossing his weapon on the ground. Harlem World then ran up on him and pistol whipped him instantly knocking him out. Seeing both goons were unconscious Harlem World grabbed each one by the ankles and dragged them to the back of the BMW, and tied them up. Then he jogged back to their minivan where Justice, and Amir were waiting.

'Bang Bang.' Harlem World knocked on the side door. Justice opened it and let him in a checked his watch. It was eight forty.

"That was fast, is everything good?" Justice asked.

"Yeah, they won't be a problem they are both tied up behind the car." Harlem World replied.

Amir just smiled already knowing his partners skill.

Just as Justice was about to speak, he glanced out the window towards the entrance of the parking lot. He saw Money-B's daughter pulling in her all silver two thousand sixteen ford mustang bumping Cardi-B. Stepping out of her Mustang she grabbed her bag then bobbed through the parking lot heading to work.

"Damn shorty bad as a mutha fucka." Amir exclaimed.

"Yeah too bad we got to snatch her ass up." Harlem World replied.

"I'd definitely holla at lil mama. She thick as hell." Amir said.

"Bruh you couldn't pull shorty if she was made out of metal and you had a magnet." Harlem World replied.

Justice busted our laughing. "Ya'll get ready." Justice ordered quieting the chatter.

"It's game time let's get it." Amir said.

As Amanda walked through the parking lot headed to work, she heard someone laughing inside of a minivan, but didn't pay it any mind. *It was probably some student.* Amanda thought to herself then in a blur the sliding door of the van shot open. Two masked men jumped out with guns pointed at her. Amanda was completely frozen in fear. All she could do is stand there as she was zipped tied then one of the mask men threw a black canvas bag over her head, then they threw her in the back of the van, and the driver pulled off.

"Whatever you do, I advise you not to say a word or I promise you your father will never see you again." Justice whispered.

"Okay please don't hurt me." Amanda pleaded.

Harlem World slapped her in the back of the head with his Glock knocking her out. Justice then searched thru her Gucci bag, and found her phone. He tried to open it up, but it was locked. Justice woke Amanda up once they were on the highway. He lifted her head covering so he could see her face.

"Open this phone, and don't try to sneak a look at me or I'll cut your eyes out." Justice spat as he handed her her phone.

Amanda punched in her password as fast as she could, and handed the phone back. Justice grabbed the phone, and scrolled through her contacts until he found what he was looking for. Then he hit the call button.

"What's up baby girl?" Money-B said after having answered on the first ring, as always when he saw his daughter's number pop up on his screen.

"Talk to your dad." Justice ordered Amanda as he held the phone out to her.

"Daddy I've been kidnapped." Amanda shouted frantically before Justice snatched the phone back.

"What the fuck." A shocked Money-B asked.

"As you can see I have something you want and care about so dearly so you'll want to pay close attention to what I have to say." Justice said.

"Mutha fucka you don't know who you're dealing wit. I'll have your head for this shit." Money-B threatened.

Justice laughed then he motioned to Harlem World. On instant Harlem World punched Amanda in her jaw. Money-B heard his daughter cry out in pain which made his stomach turn knowing that shit was more serious than he had thought.

"See that wasn't smart of you making all those threats. We're just getting started here. I want you to understand you're not in the driver's seat. I make the demands, and you listen that's how this works." Justice instructed.

"I'm listening." Money-B shot back.

"Good, I want you to pay close attention." Justice replied letting what he said hang in the air before he continued.

"If you call the police or try to have this number traced, your daughter will be killed. Do you understand?" Justice asked.

"Yes." Money-B answered with defeat in his voice.

"I'll call later." Justice stated before hanging up the phone.

After some what a peaceful drive Amir finally reached Mt. Airy. He exited off the Cook School Road exit and continued to navigate through downtown. Then he made a right onto West

Lebanon Street after a few more minutes of driving he had finally reached Justice brother's warehouse. Amir pulled the minivan to the back of the parking lot. Justice got out and punched the entrance code in then opened the door shooting back to the van to retrieve Amanda. Amir and Harlem World hopped out with Justice leading the way the crew ushered Amanda inside. Justice took her straight to the warehouse office where the monitors, and cameras where set up, and hooked to a small laptop which was wired up for a live feed. Justice sat Amanda in the office chair facing the cameras, then he tied her hands to the office desk, and walked around to the laptop, and punched some numbers in. Amir and Harlem World looked on surprised at what they were seeing.

"I want you to pay attention Amanda. You're not the one we want. If your father plays by the rules, I swear on my dead son you'll be ok. If he doesn't you'll be collateral damage. Each time your father doesn't meet one of our demands, you'll lose a finger." Justice stated as he pulled the canvas bag off Amanda's head before continuing. "I'll try to make this as easy as possible you can go home with all ten fingers and toes still intact or... you already know the rest. Your fate is in your fathers hands." Justice stated then he picked up a pair of bolt cutters, and walked out of the office pulling his phone from his pocket he called Kanden.

'Ring' 'Ring'.

"Yeah what's good lil bruh?" Kanden said answering on the second ring.

"The first part of my plan is underway. We have Money-B's daughter."

"Okay good. I don't really want her hurt but." Kanden paused. "Fuck it you handle it the best way you see fit. Just make sure everything is cleaned up nice and tidy when you're finished." Kanden voiced.

"Aite there'll be some blowback, but I'll take the necessary steps to ensure that Money-B is dead. He'll have to give himself up in order to secure his daughter's safety. If not then the girl's dead and I'll have to hunt him another way." Justice said.

"Keep me posted lil bruh." Kanden ordered.

"Got cha." Justice confirmed then he hung the phone up and walked back inside.

Thoughts of his sister Zeenah and how his grandmother didn't tell him the whole truth came to his mind still not understanding why he was doing this. He knew he was doing this more for his family than himself, *maybe it was for the money fuck it. It was too late to question his own actions now.* He thought to himself.

"Yo bruh." Amir interrupted Justices thoughts.

"Yeah what's up?" Justice inquired.

"If you wanna take off, I can take care of this part of the plan." Amir offered.

"Nah I'm good bruh. You know I wouldn't ask you to do something that I wouldn't do myself. Plus I have to be here just in case there's any blow back. We're still somewhat on Money-B's turf." Justice replied.

"Then we're all staying, because I'm not leaving you here alone." Amir stated.

"Neither am I." Harlem World said.

"This shit is about to get crazy. He'll have all his goons beating the bushes and hitting the streets our ace in the hole is that he doesn't know who we are and that buys us a little time, so we gotta strike now while he's torn with emotions." Justice replied.

"You wanta put the other plan in motion?" Inquired Amir with a raised eyebrow.

"Yeah put Hawk on that shit he's dying to get his hands dirty. Give him the account eraser back, and tell Hawk I want Money-B naked like a bitch in the strip club." Justice ordered. "Aite let's get this show on the road."

Amir agreed while rubbing his hands together, Harlem World stood in the corner gripping his AR. Justice walked over to the dial pad and punched in Money-B's number then he hit the button which turned on the monitor and the camera. Money-B picked up on the second ring with his image popping up on the monitor.

Money-B answered his phone, and out of nowhere an image appeared on his phone of his daughter with a masked man standing next to her. It was a live video Money-B took a deep breath knowing that these weren't amateurs that he was dealing wit. "Whoever you are I'll give you whatever you want." Money-B answered.

"Alright, now that you're acting respectful." Justice replied with menace in his voice as he stared at the camera he was pleased from seeing the expression written on Money-B's face.

"You've been muscling in on my associate's turfs. AS of right now." Justice paused for effect. "You're going to call Kanden and give him control over all your spots. On Martin Luther King, Devonshire, Clara Cox, everything in Mount Airy, Winston and Charlotte. I want you out of North Carolina. You're going to call your lieutenants and tell them to shut down operations and leave me whatever work and money you have." Justice ordered.

"So Kanden's behind this. I'll tell you what. I'll triple whatever he's paying you. Money is not a problem I assure you." Money-B replied.

"I thought you were a smart man to at least have the common sense to know that this is not a negotiable situation. Since you're not I'ma have to teach you a valuable lesson." Justice stated walking over to a table, and picking up a pair of heavy duty bolt cutters. Then he strolled over to Amanda like he didn't have a care in the world. He grabbed her left hand placing her index finger in between the bolt cutter blades, then he squeezed the handles together. The sound of ligament and bone being cut was deafening.

"Aaaargh oh my God." Amanda bellowed in excruciating pain.

"Please stop." Amanda continued to cry out as blood squirted from her hand.

Staring at his phone Money-B's face turned white as he was forced to watch his daughter's finger being cut off. He was lost and didn't know what to do.

"Okay, okay please don't hurt my baby girl. What the fuck do you want?" a fully defeated Money-B shouted frantically. And continued to scream in his phone at the masked man.

"I told you what I wanted. It's your job to make it happen. And I hope for Amanda's sake you understand that because she's only got nine fingers left." Justice stated. "I know you got your goons all over the triad looking for us, but rest assure you won't find us. Make no mistake about it this lovely woman is here because of you, and she will die because of you. The only way she comes out of this alive, is if you trade places with her. If you do this, I promise that you won't ever be an afterthought in these streets, but your daughter will live. The ball is in your court. Whatever happens to her is on you." Justice explained.

"You win." Money-B whispered.

"I'll call you with further demands." Justice stated before he shut the laptop down.

When the phone disconnected, and his screen went black Money-B paced back and forth going over every possible scenario in his head. The only thought that kept coming up was that someone was going to die. He wanted the kidnappers, but he would have to settle for Kanden. If he had to die Kanden would suffer the same fate. Knowing his baby girl was in danger filled him with dread. If need be he would dive on the knife, but not before he exhausted all of his vast resources available to him.

Angrily Money-B punched in Rondo's number, after what seemed like an eternity, but was actually only forty-five seconds. Finally Rondo answered on the third ring.

"Yo what's good?"

"What's good? What's good is Kanden had his people snatch my baby girl up." A frustrated Money-B shouted hysterically.

"I need you to get down here now." Money-B demanded. Irritated and perplexed at how he had got caught slipping. He wondered what happened to the goons he sent to keep her safe. *They better be dead if not they will be.* Money-B thought to himself.

"Where are you?"

"In Charlotte."

"I'm on the way." Rondo replied.

Money-B hung up wishing that Amanda had listened to him when he had wanted to send her off to go to school out of state, but she was adamant about staying close to home. Knowing it was his fault because he had agreed. Thinking he was untouchable because he was King Charles' grandson. Honestly he didn't think Kanden would come at him this hard involving family in their war. King Charles had warned him, but he didn't listen, and now he regretted not taking the old man's advice. He wanted to call him and ask for his help, but he couldn't it was too early in the game for him to be asking for his help. It would be a sign of weakness on his part, as a down south boss. Money-B took a shot of Henny then leaned back in his chair and closed his eyes. He needed to get himself together, and he needed to do it quickly before everything he loved and held dear was lost.

The next day Money-B still didn't have the answer for his current problem, and Rondo didn't show up last night which was unlike him, but it was no telling where Rondo was when he had called him last night. *He would call him in a few.* Money-B thought to himself. But first he need to make the most important call right now which was to Kanden. Maybe he could reason with him or at least buy himself some time. He felt like his life was unraveling one thread at a time. He couldn't believe how crazy shit was going. But one thing he did know somebody was going to bleed for what they did to his baby girl Money-B thought to himself. As he unlocked his phone he scrolled through his contacts until he found Kanden's number then hit the call button.

'Ring.'

"Money-B I should feel honored. I've been waiting for your call." Kanden said answering on the first ring.

"We didn't have to do this Kanden."

"Oh we definitely did." Kanden replied.

"Look, I give you control over all my spots. Can we just keep our beef between us?" Money-B asked.

"Bruh, I was never beefing with you in the first place. We could've all ate off the same plate, but you're greedy, and you're grimy. You thought you could make your own rules. You let King Charles put a battery in your back stirring up old family beefs."

"Fuck all this bullshit. You have my daughter, you crossed the line with this one."

"There are no lines when it comes to war. King Charles should have taught you that. And by the way thanks for the gift." Kanden replied and then hung up.

Hearing the dial tone Money-B put his face in his hands. When he looked he saw Rondo walking into his office.

"What took you so long?" Money-B asked.

"One of my soldiers caught one of the guys responsible for the hit at Clara Cox. I spent the night working him over. I need to see what I could get out of him." Rondo replied.

"Tell me what was his name and what did you find out." Money-B asked.

"For starters his name was Gunz. He ran a small crew for Kanden. He didn't know too much, but he told me that Kanden has a brother name Justice who's supposed to be taken over for Kanden if he can end this war."

"A brother." Kanden has no brother. Money-B thought deeply to himself. "Look I want you to find out who this Justice is and I want you to slump his ass, and everyone around him. Second,

I want you to make the streets bleed at all cost. Kanden thinking I'm turning over all my spots, he has another thing coming. He wants a war I'm bout to turn the triad into Sparta, and he's done woke up Leonidas. Third get my baby back A.S.A. fucking P. Now get out and don't come back unless you have my baby girl."

"I'm on it Mikal, Amanda is family to me also." Rondo replied then he turned and walked out.

Agent Slade pulled up at the crime scene in his F-350 and got out. The streets were full of police that were securing the crime scene on Florida Street a body had been thrown out near the convenience store. The owner's son found the body and called the police. When Agent Slade ducked under the crime scene yellow tape he walked over to the dead body that was covered up, and surrounded by two detectives. He flashed his F.B.I. badge.

"I'm Agent Slade."

"How are you? I'm Detective Garner, and this here is Detective Martian."

"What do we have here?" Agent Slade asked.

"The deceased is a black male early thirties his name is Larry Cannon, he went by the name of Gunz he ran a crew for the Santiago family."

Hearing that news Agent Slade bent down and pulled the sheet to see the deceased face. He did not recognize the man, but this was more evidence to support his theory of a family war uprising.

Agent Slade stood up. "Do you have any leads?"

"Not right now. What we know is that he was killed somewhere else, and then dumped here." Detective Garner replied.

"We need to find out where he was murdered at. I have a hunch why he was dumped here." Agent Slade stated.

"I would like to know sir. What you have in mind. We need any lead that we can get." Detective Martian stated.

"Okay for starters this is Santiago's turf no one would dare lift a finger let alone kill him here. Mr. Cannon led a crew correct?" Agent Slade asked.

"Correct." Detective Garner answered.

"Then his body being dumped here is a message." Agent Slade stated.

"A message to who?" Detective Martian asked.

"That is what I am going to find out." Agent Slade said as he walked back to his truck.

Justice, Amir, and Harlem World remained at the warehouse guarding Money-B's daughter. After the video message Justice had untied Amanda from the desk and tended to her wounded hand. Once he had her fixed up and was certain that she wouldn't bleed out, he had sent Harlem World out to bring some food back. After Money-B's daughter was fed Justice locked her in a small room with a mattress and a set of bed covers. Amir had stayed up on guard while Justice and Harlem World slept.

When Justice had awaken he looked at his phone, and seen that he had an unread text from his brother Kanden.

"Call me ASAP." Was all the text said. Justice then checked his watch it was 10:30 am.

"Shit we over slept. Amir go check on Amanda, see if she needs some new bandages." Justice asked then walked off and dialed his brother's number.

'Ring' 'Ring'.

"Justice." Kanden answered.

"Yeah."

"I'm glad you called me early." Kanden replied.

"What is it, what's going on?" Justice asked.

"One of my soldiers was snatched up last night. He was tortured, they dumped his body in Greensboro as a message to me."

"Okay so what's the issue? What does that have to do with what I'm doing here?" Justice asked.

"My top soldiers know who you are, and that you are taking over after me. To be safe I'm assuming that he gave your name up."

"What the fuck you mean gave my name up?" Justice asked.

"What I mean is you need to wrap this shit up, because if Money-B finds out who you are everybody around you may be in trouble." Kanden spat.

"Aite I'm bout to put some speed on this shit. Thanks on the heads up."

"No problem."

Justice hung up then walked over to Amir and Harlem World. "It's been a change of plan." Justice informed.

"What happened?" Amir asked.

"Money-B may know who I am."

"I don't understand how could he know?" Harlem World asked.

"One of Kanden's men was snatched up late last night, he may have spilled the beans. Amir I want you to hit Red Bull and have him and Halftime keep an eye on my grandma, my sister, and Lisa." Justice said.

"I got cha." Amir answered immediately pulling out his phone.

"In the meantime I'm bout to speed this shit up." Justice said.

"I'm wit it." Harlem World state facts.

Justice pull out his phone again, and this time he called Money-B.

'Ring'.

"Hello." Money-B answered on the first ring.

"It's time to pay the piper mutha fucka." Justice spat.

"Young blood what's all the hostility for, I've spoken to Kanden. I let him know I'm turning my spots over to him. This is a process. It can't happen in one night or day." Money-B said.

"Fuck all that stalling shit. I know you're trying to find out who I am. I'll take your turf when you're dead. We make the swap today."

"Today it is then, but I want to know who it is I'm turning

myself over to. Is your name Justice." Money-B asked.

The phone went silent and Justice was caught off guard by hearing Money-B say his name.

"Yeah that's your name, so you are looking to take over after your brother huh. I didn't even know he had one. He must have hidden you under a rock somewhere out of state."

"Enough of the bullshit. You meet me today or your daughter dies."

"Come on man, don't go all gun ho on me. Where do you want to meet?" Money-B asked.

"Bring your ass to the old J.J. Jones Auditorium you have two hours. Come alone any tricks your daughter will die." Justice spat then hung the phone up.

"Everything is in order I let Red Bull know what's up. How did it go with Money-B?" Amir asked.

"He has two hours to meet me at the old J. J. Jones Auditorium." Justice replied.

"Why so fast?"

"We gotta show him we ain't playing games. He knows my name. He said it, so we have to strike before he can send someone to hit the streets for information."

"Okay what's the plan?" Amir asked.

"Money-B is not stupid. I know he won't come alone. He'll have someone follow him. It's a park next to the auditorium. It's a path that you can take that will lead you right to it. You'll be able to see anybody that pulls up. If you spot anyone I want you to take them out." Justice explained.

"When you want me to post up?" Amir asked.

"I need you to head that way now and take the walkie talkie. We need to stay a step ahead of Money-B." Justice replied.

"What you need me to do?" Harlem World asked.

"You're going to take the girl you'll release her when I give you the signal."

"So I'll be with you."

"Yeah you'll be with me now let's suit up and get ready. We

have two hours let's make them count." Justice stated.

As soon as Money-B ended his call with Justice he immediately called Rondo.

'Ring' 'Ring'.

"Yes." Rondo answered.

"You were right about Kanden's brother. Justice is the one who has my daughter." Money-B said.

"You sure."

"Yeah, I said his name then it was instant silence. He moved up the date he wants to make the swap in two hours." Money-B explained.

"You can't do that, not until we find out everything about him. I have our best digging up everything they can we still need time, can you stall him."

"No it won't work. I can't risk him killing Amanda."

"Okay tell me the location we'll jump the drop."

"No I'm not risking Amanda. I'ma send someone ahead of me to pop him. If I don't make it back you kill everyone around Justice. I am positive that he is our guy."

"Alright I'll handle things the way you asked, but I feel like it's a better way."

"I know you do but this has to be done right. I'll keep in touch." Money-B said and then hung up.

After hanging up with Rondo Money-B called one of his soldiers named Bo-Loc and gave him the rundown of what he wanted him to do. Then after hanging up he text him the address to the meeting place with instructions to kill anyone he saw. After putting his plan together he dreaded making the last call to the person he needed to call most. Money-B stared at his phone for a lil while before he dialed King Charles number pressing the call button the phone began to ring.

'Ring' 'Ring' 'Ring'.

"Talk." King Charles said when he answered sounding fairly weak.

"Grandfather." Money-B replied feeling kinda worried at hearing the weakness in his grandpa's voice.

"Hey Mikal, I was just thinking about you. I wanted to apologize to you about what happened the other day." King Charles said.

"It's okay grandpa, I know you are under a lot of stress having to go to those treatments 3 or 4 times a week."

"Yeah, I'm feeling weak now. I wish your grandmother was here to take care of me. She's the only woman I really every loved. It's just us now." King Charles replied and then began to cry. "Mikal you're all I have left. You have to take care of things, you have to be strong." King Charles said through sobs.

"I will grandpa. I will destroy the Santiago family for taking my mother and grandmother away from us."

"That's it grandson, you sound like a Sanderson now."

"I just found out that Kanden has a brother named Justice."

"Yeah that's Danielle's son. I seen him once when he was a baby."

"Well he just entered the battlefield. He kidnapped Amanda and wants me to trade my life for hers."

"He did what, I told you to protect your family."

"I will make no excuses, I will get her back, I promise you grandpa, it's all arranged."

"You better that's my great grandbaby. I don't want to have to get involved, but I will if I have to. I'm just not the man I used to be. But I still have a lot of power at my disposal." King Charles replied.

"I know grandpa, like I said I'll take care of this."

"Okay grandson keep me posted. I gotta go I need some rest."

"Talk to you later grandpa, I love you man."

"Love you too Mikal." King Charles replied and then hung up.

After his conversation with his grandfather Money-B knew what he had to do and was okay with it. He gently laid his phone down and prayed that Bo-Loc would get the job done.

"On the road to riches and diamond rings real niggas do real things." Amir sang along to the classic Kool G rap song Road to Riches. Pulling into the ball field parking lot of the old J.J. Jones School in Justice's SUV. Amir lights a pre-rolled spliff and takes a deep satisfying pull, exhaling the smoke he sat the blunt back down in the ashtray, and screws a silencer onto his nickel plated forty-four bulldog. Slowly he opened the door and got out of the Jeep he looked around to make sure he wasn't seen. When he was satisfied he walked over and sat at a picnic table and waited.

Ten minutes later a black two thousand and seventeen Chevy Camaro pulls into the abandon parking lot bumping Gucci Man's Trap House. Amir tosses the roach from his blunt and creeps towards the dumpsters knowing that someone would probably park next to Justice Jeep. Amir wanted to be sure he had a straight line to the driver side of the Camaro. As he looked on he saw the interior light inside the Camaro come on indicating that the door was ajar. Amir smiled to himself knowing that even from thirty yards he couldn't miss if he choose to take the shot. AS he continued to look on he saw a heavy set man get out of the Camaro. Seeing this Amir took off in a full sprint pulling up the forty-four at the same time. Running up on his prey at point blank range he squeeze his bulldog.

Pft, pft, pft, pft.

Instantly dropping the heavy set man Amir bent down to check his pulse to be sure he was dead. Then he reached inside his pocket and pulled out a pair of latex gloves. He put them on and began to search the body grabbing the guy's keys and his phone. Surprised that the phone didn't have a lock he scrolled through the call log and seen that Money-B was the last person that the dead man had called. Satisfied he put the guy's phone in his pocket. Amir then walked over to the Camaro and popped the trunk then he walked back over to the body bent down and grabbed both of the dead guy's ankles and dragged him back to the Camaro and threw him inside the trunk and closed it. When he got back to his jeep he saw that Justice had a gas can in the back. Amir grabbed it and walked back to the Camaro opened the gas can and pours gas inside the Camaro then on the hood, roof, and trunk as he walked back to the Jeep he tilted the gas can and pours a line as he walked then he put the top back on the can and set it back where he had gotten it. Pulling a cigarette from his pocket and a pack of matches. Amir lit his cigarette then let the lit match fall to the ground. Instantly the black Camaro was engulfed in flames. Amir got back inside the Jeep.

"Set di fire pon di wicked mon. He a hot boy for real. Word to Juvie." Amir laughed to himself at his fake Jamaican accent as he pulled out of the parking lot watching the smoke from his rear-view mirror as he headed back to the warehouse to meet Justice.

Getting impatient waiting on Amir to call and let him know what's up. Justice pulls out his phone and calls Lisa.

'Ring' 'Ring' 'Ring'.

"Hey baby." Lisa answered.

"Hey love, what you doing?" Justice asked.

"Thinking about you."

"I was thinking about you too, is everything alright?"

"Yeah baby everything's fine. Your friend Red Bull came by."

"Is he still there?"

"Yeah he's sitting in his car outside."

"What's going on baby, talk to me?"

"Get your 380, and keep it close to you, matter of fact get in the car with Red Bull and leave the house."

"Baby what the fuck is going on?"

"There may be people looking for me. Just get somewhere safe stay with Red Bull. That's all I have time to say right now. I'll call you later. Love you."

"Love you too please be careful."

"I will." Justice replied and then hung up and began to check his AR. When he looked up and seen Harlem World letting Amir back inside.

"What happened, why are you back already?" Justice asked.

"The guy Money-B sent is dead laying in the truck of his car burning by now." Amir replied.

"You set him on fire?" Justice asked.

"Yeah wanted to make sure there were no evidence." Amir answered. "I got his phone tho and guess who was the last person that he called." Amir quizzed while giving Justice pound.

"Let me guess Money-B." Justice replied.

"This muthafucka thinks we're playing. Let's kill that bitch, and show him we ain't playing." Harlem World spat wanting to get shit over wit.

"No we're not going to kill her. Unless we have to, but I'ma show Money-B this ain't no game." Justice said as he walked away headed to Amanda's room with the dead man's phone in his hand.

Reaching Amanda's room he snatched the door open after he slid his mask back over his face.

Seeing the door being snatched open Amanda ran to the corner of the room and balled up. "Lil mama your pops think we playing. I believe he thinks your life is indispensable. We have to show him we mean business." Justice spoke with all seriousness then he began looking thru the dead man's phone until he found Money-B's number then he pressed the call button.

"Yo is everything taking care of?" Money-B asked wanting to get straight to the point.

"Mutha fucka you think this is a game huh?" Justice angrily inquired.

"Wha… What, how did you get that phone?" Money-B asked.

"I'm ten moves ahead. You got one hour to decide your life or your daughters."

"Daddy help me please." Amanda cried out in the background.

"One hour mutha fucka or I'ma mail you her head in a box." Justice said and then hung up.

Chapter 10

Where Ya At

Money-B's plan didn't work. It was time to throw in the towel, before he got his daughter killed. Money-B thought to himself. He had to admit Justice Santiago was smarter than he was willing to give credit for. The whole while he had been a step ahead knowing his moves before he could execute them. This was nothing but karma coming back to bite him in the ass. He had been doing all his dirt searching for something that truly didn't matter to him, and in the process he had lost focus and by doing so he put Amanda's life in danger. She didn't deserve this she deserve better and as her father he had to protect her. Even if it meant giving his life to do so. Hearing his daughter cry out in the back ground of her captors had broken something inside of him that couldn't be welded back together.

"Fuck." Money-B shouted after taking an unhealthy swig of

the Hennesey XO he favored. Angrily he punched in Rondo's number and hit send.

"What up bruh." Rondo answered on the first ring.

"I need you to come to the mansion right now." Money-B spat.

"Aite let me drop this female off and I'm on the way."

"Fuck dat kick her ass out, who's paying your ass me or her?" Money-B stated with authority.

"Aite I'm on the way now."

"You got fifteen minutes or I swear to God I'll kill you myself." Money-B threatened meaning every word as he hung up.

Ten minutes later Rondo walked through the door, without saying a word he strolled over to Money-B bar and picked up the half empty bottle of Henny and poured himself a drink.

"I swear to God Money. I can't seem to get a bead on this nigga it's like he popped up outta nowhere." Rondo said after taking a sip of his drink.

"His whole name is Justice Santiago. We have been focusing our efforts in the wrong area. Instead of Greensboro check further down. I'm pretty sure his name will pop up then." Money-B said as he picked up his keys and toss them to Rondo. "Here you got the keys to the whip now." Money-B said.

"Yo hold up." Rondo replied as he caught the keys in the air. He tried to decline the offer.

"It's too late. I hollered at old Sammy and made arrangements. My grandfather won't deal with you because you're not his kinfolk. If he does you'll have to go thru my daughter. Sammy will take care of you everything's been taken care of." Money-B spoke with the authority of the street general he was.

"On my momma Mikal. I will avenge you even if it means my life. He will feel pain before this is over." Rondo vow.

"I know Bruh, but right now I have to get Amanda back and make things right with her. I hope you can understand that. But if not you will when you have children." Money-B spoke as his emotions made his voice crack.

"I've also transferred my money into three accounts yours, Amanda's, and my wife Kaci." Money-B finished referring to his wife of twenty years.

"Damn I never thought it would end like this, I thought we'd retire." Rondo replied.

"You're a street general like myself it's no way you ever truly believed that with all the dirt we've done over the years. Karmas a fast bitch. I couldn't out run her. You know how it go, you do dirt you get dirt." Money-B stated with remorse written in his voice. "I've left a letter with detailed instructions for the young wolves concerning who to bring up in ranks. It's in my desk locked away you already have the key. One more thing my friend. I want you to turn the motherfucking heat up after I'm gone." Money-B ordered grabbing Rondo in a brotherly love embrace before picking up his keys to his two thousand and sixteen Lamborghini and the rest of the Henny and headed out the door. Once outside his mansion Money-B called his wife after he got in his Lambo.

'Ring,' 'Ring,' 'Ring'.

"Hello." Kaci answered.

"Hey baby. I just wanted you to know how sorry I am, and how much I love you. Don't worry you'll be taken care of." Money-B said nearly breaking down from the emotional roller coaster the family had been on the last couple of days.

"It's okay honey. I love you too, but please whatever you do get our baby back." Kaci replied.

"I will, I promise you she'll call she she's safe."

"Okay." Kaci answered and then hung up.

Money-B looked at the picture of his wife on his phone, sadden that he'll never see her again. After he ended his call he flipped thru his call log and called Justice.

'Ring.

"Yo." Justice answered.

"I'm in the car now. I'm coming from Charlotte, so it'll take me a lil time to get to you. But I'm on the way. Just keep your word and let my baby go, where do you want to meet?" A fully defeated Money-B asked.

Justice could hear the fear in Money-B's voice, so he knew that he was telling the truth.

"Alright your precious baby girl will be dropped as soon as you're spotted. Get on the highway. I'll text you the location in ten minutes. You know what's at stake, so don't play no games. Any funny business on your end and the girls dead." Justice reiterated before hanging up.

Justice hung up on Money-B and then turned to Amir and Harlem World.

"A yo it's game time, Amir you take Amanda in the van. We'll tie her up and throw her in the back. Don't do anything extra until I give you the word. Harlem World you'll be with me." Justice said then he text Money-B the location. After receiving the confirmation text back that Money-B knew where to go. He and Amir went and grabbed Amanda tied her up and escorted her to the van. Justice gave Amir the address then he bent down and placed a detonator under the van.

"What's the detonator for?" Amir asked.

"If shit hits the fan and Money-B play games, once you are clear I'ma blow the van with her in it. Keep your walkie talkie on you I have the controller with me. Stay close if you're out of range the controller won't work. Pray we won't need this. Lord knows I don't want to hurt the girl." Justice replied as he dapped Amir up and then watched him pull off.

Justice and Harlem World grabbed their AR's and hopped inside Justices SUV and headed to the meeting place following closely behind Amir. After a twenty minute drive still in Mount Airy they pulled onto Simmons Road and headed towards Sadies Court Memorium, Amir parks the van in the parking lot and grabbed his AR off the passenger seat saying his goodbyes to Amanda he exits the van and finds a nice hiding spot where he had a view from above. The tree he had climbed was comfortable enough for him to his position he checked his AR making sure the beam worked for the range he was currently at. When he was sure he radioed Justice with his walkie talkie.

"I'm in position." Amir stated.

"Copy that, stay ready. You see any movement you take them out." Justice replied.

After a forty minute wait a black Lamborghini pulled into Sadies Court and parked and flicked it's lights. Justice flicked his lights in return then him and Harlem World got out of the Jeep AR's in hand. Money-B stepped out of the Lambo on wobbly legs due to the excessive drinking and leaned on his whip. Five seconds later a red dot appeared on his chest Money-B threw his hands up in surrender.

"I am here as promised. Where is my daughter? I want to see her, you gave me your word Justice." Money-B hollered.

Justice pulled the detonator from his coat pocket and held it up. "She's in the van go to her and cut her loose. If you make any sudden moves once she is cut loose. I will blow the van." Justice replied and then waved his AR towards the van indicating for Money-B to walk to it.

Money-B followed the silent instructions, and slowly walked to the van then slide the side door open and climbed inside. Father and daughter both were overwhelmed with emotion at their reunion. Money-B reached and grabbed the knife that was left on the floor. He cut Amanda loose Amanda hugged her father like she never did before.

"I am glad you are safe."

"I'm so afraid daddy."

"Don't be baby everything is okay here take my phone. When you leave here call your mother and let her know you are safe."

"What about you daddy?"

"I have to go with these guys."

"I don't want you to go."

"I have to it's the only way to guarantee your safety. Grow strong little one and when you are at your strongest avenge me. I will always be here." Money-B said pointing to his daughter's heart. Money-B looked up as he heard Justice calling his name.

"Okay it's time to go home. I love you Amanda."

"I love you too daddy." Amanda replied as they both got out of the van.

"Alright old man times up." Justice said as he watched Money-B and his daughter get out of the van.

"We are here, what now?" Money-B asked.

"The girl can walk away. I want you to walk towards me." Justice hollered.

Money-B hugged his daughter one last time, then he told her to run away and he slowly walked towards Justice.

Justice smiled to himself as he and Harlem World walked to meet Money-B

"So you are the infamous Money-B."

"And you must be Justice Santiago."

"Now that the introductions are out of the way you must be wondering why you have been targeted?" Justice asked.

"No young man, I already know that Kanden is behind this. The question is, do you know why you are doing this?" Money-B said.

"Because it must be done that is all I need to know."

"Spoken like a true Santiago."

"Enough talk, turn around, and put your hands behind your back." Justice ordered.

Money-B complied and turned around while Harlem World zipped tied him. Once confined Justice hit Money-B in the back of his head with the butt of his AR knocking Money-B unconscious. Justice then pulled out his walkie talkie and radioed Amir.

"Aite let's get out of here and head home."

"Copy that." Amir replied then he climbed down the tree.

Justice and Harlem World dragged Money-B to their Jeep and threw him in the back. Once Money-B was secured Amir walked up joining his crew.

"That was a piece of cake." Amir stated.

"Yeah like taking candy from a baby." Harlem World replied.

"Let's get outta here, Amir, you and Harlem World take my Jeep I'ma grab Money-B's Lambo I'll follow ya'll back to the warehouse."

"Aite bro let's roll." Amir replied as he jumped in the driver seat of Justice Suburban. Harlem World followed suite while Justice got inside Money-B's Lambo both cars pulled off heading back to the warehouse.

Amanda ran like her life depended on it and only stopped when she was sure that she was a long way away from her kidnappers. When she did she pulled out her father's phone and scroll thru his contacts until she landed on Rondo's number then she pressed the call button. Rondo thinking it was Money-B picked up on the first ring.

"Yo." Rondo answered.

"Rondo they have my father. You have to get here quick and save him they're going to kill him."

"Amanda is that you?"

"Yes Rondo."

"You're free, where are you?"

"I don't know, did you hear what I said, they have my dad."

"Calm down kid go find a store or someone that can tell you where you are. When you find out call me back and I'll be on my way."

"Okay." Amanda replied hanging the phone up and began

looking around.

When Justice and his crew arrived back at the warehouse both cars pulled around the back and parked. Justice got out first bragging bout how smooth the Lambo had ridden. Then he walked to the warehouse door and punched in the code. The lock popped open. Justice slung the door open then went inside and rolled a small tire to the door and leaned it against the door so it would stay open. Walking back to his SUV he helped Amir and Harlem World carry Money-B inside. Then strapped him down to the same chair that still had his daughter's blood on it. Harlem World walked back outside to retrieve their AR's. Justice pulled out his phone and called his brother.

Ring, Ring, Ring.

"Talk to me lil bruh." Kanden answered.

"I have the package." Justice stated.

"Good, that's exactly what I was hoping to hear. I'll be there in thirty minutes. Don't do nothing until I get there." Kanden said.

"Bet." Justice confirmed before hanging up.

"Wake this nigga up my brother's on the way." Justice said to Amir.

Amir walked over to Money-B and began to slap him lightly until he opened his eyes.

Money-B tried to move until he realized that he was tied up.

"What the fuck you want from me?" Money-B shouted trying to buy himself some time.

Justice bent down, so close that Money-B could smell his breath. "I want your life. I can't be bought or bargained with." Justice whispered.

"Well get it over wit pussy boy." Money-B replied.

Justice began to laugh just as Harlem World walked back inside the warehouse office.

"What's so funny big bruh?" Harlem World asked.

"This guy here he funnier than Kevin Hart. Pass me that blunt bruh." Justice said as he took a deep pull of the spliff.

"How the hell this guy end up running the mid-south?" Harlem World asked.

"One thing for sho he don't have to worry about running it no more." Justice stated comically.

"Do ya'll even know who my grandfather is?" Money-B asked.

"Mutha fucka we don't give two flying fucks who he is." Amir shot back.

"Well Kanden knowns who he is and he will kill you when he finds out about this." Money-B replied. "I swear on my daughter on that."

"If it was up to me ya whole family would be dead, then you wouldn't have shit to swear on believe me when I tell you that." Justice spat as his lifted his AR pointing the barrel at Money-B's face.

"Chill lil bruh." Kanden said as he walked in the office with two body guards by his side. He touched the barrel of Justices AR lowering it with his hand. "Not yet I want to speak with him first."

Justice took a step back.

"Honestly I can't believe your soft ass was able to pull this off." Money-B spat.

"Why did you start this war Mikal?" Kanden asked.

"Your family took my mother and grandmother from me, our beef is eternal. I'll see you in hell when this is over. It won't be long until you join me, my grandfather will have you all killed."

"So that's it, that's all you have to say to me?" Kanden asked.

"Fuck you go ahead and do what you do. I'm ready I'm at peace with this." Money-B spat.

"Lil bruh you had a task to complete and you did it you're in the driver seat now and with that the opportunity to make millions of dollars. The ball's in your court you've made me proud." Kanden stated while looking each of Justices soldiers in the eyes before continuing. "I want ya'll to remember one thing before

I go." Kanden paused before stating. "Loyalty and respect are the two most important things to have in this game. Even more important than money and fear. If people fear you they'll do anything to get you out the way. On that note Justice finish the job." Kanden said before turning his back, and leaving the warehouse with his two goons in tow.

"Gladly." Justice replied with a wolf eating sheep grin before raising his AR-15, and pulling the trigger leaving Money-B slumped.

"Yo Amir you and Harlem. I want ya'll to take Money-B's body, and dump it in the middle of Clara Cox, and let everybody know playtime is over." Justice gave clear instructions before leaving the warehouse in Money-B Lambo.

Chapter 11

Dead Men Don't Talk

Rondo had finally found Amanda and picked her up after she found out where she was by stumbling on to a small neighborhood store. The store clerk had given her the exact location then she had called Rondo back. It took him a little over an hour to reach her, when he did he took her straight to the hospital where he had spent hours in the waiting room waiting for her. They had to stitch her finger up. When she came out her hand was wrapped in a huge bandage. Neither of them said a word as Rondo threw a blanket around her shoulders and took her home to see her mother.

When Rondo woke up the next morning he sat at Money-B's office chair with his keys on the table. There was still no word of Money-B, Rondo remembered the letter that Money-B said he had written. Grabbing the keys off the table he found the key to the desk drawer and opened it up. As soon as he did he saw the letter and picked it up and began to read.

If you are reading this Rondo that must mean that I am dead. Then that means you are in charge now. You are my daughter's protector now. Show her the game, as I showed it to you. When she is ready turn her loose on the Santiago's show no mercy on them. Raise BG in the ranks to take your old position. He is the most capable of all the wolves. Tell my grandfather that I love him and I did all I could and that I am sorry for letting his down. I could not let them kill my daughter she is my angel, she is the best of me. Until we meet again my friend keep your head down and your rifle up.

After Rondo finished reading Money-B's letter he wiped his face brushing away the tears that had fallen. Then he picked up the phone and began to dial King Charles number.

Harlem World and Amir bared off the exit that would take them to High Point. They rode in a white utility work van that Harlem World had stolen. Money-B's dead body laid in the back wrapped in a tarp and rolled up inside a carpet. They were on a mission to make a statement of the current change of power. After entering High Point it wasn't long until they reached Clara Cox.

"Yo get ready for the drop off." Amir said turning into the hood of Clara Cox.

"I'm ready." Harlem World replied.

Slowly creeping down Lake Street it was a lil past 12:00. There was plenty of activity going on, fiends getting served, prostitutes tricking and a few people chilling in front of different houses with so many different vehicles flowing through nobody paid any attention to the white utility work van that had stopped in the middle of the street. Harlem World slid the sliding door open Amir hurried to the back then they both jumped out and tossed Money-B's body on the ground.

"This is a important message to all the trappers in the hood." Harlem World hollered making sure he had the attention of all those in ear shot before he continued.

"There's about to be a serious drought and this package is a return to sender. I hope this shows how serious it's going to get. I'd like to thank everyone for listening."

Harlem World finished then kicked Money-B's body and laughed to himself while he jumped back inside the van. Amir pulled off burning the tires in the middle of the road.

"What the fuck?" an onlooker asked.

"Who was that in that van?" asked another as people gathered around the body.

Dope boys were daring one another to open the rolled carpet to see who the unlucky soul was. The crowd began to get bigger some offered money trying to entice someone to peek inside.

"Yo I got a twenty for whoever looks first." Dared one dope boy.

"Shit I got a sixteenth." Dared another.

"I'll give whoever open that shit up a hundred dollars." A big mouth by stander added dropping a crisp hundred dollar bill in the hat that was being passed around.

"Fuck that I'm getting that money." A gapped tooth crackhead named Jean hollered. Brazenly walking up to the carpet not giving a fuck. She took of her shirt revealing a pair of sagging titties.

"Oh cover them damn saddle bags up." Someone shouted.

"Fuck you, I'll be on the moon in a minute." Jean talked shit as she began to unroll the carpet.

"Who is it?" Someone asked.

"Damn let me look." Jean stopped in midsentence and stood with her mouth hung wide open. The recognition of the body hit her like a Mack dump truck.

"Oh my God." Jean said staggering backwards.

"It's Money-B." Jean reveal a little over a whisper still frozen in place.

"Girl you better quit playing." Someone hollered.

"I'm not playing." Jean replied grabbing the hat and pocketing her winnings and getting ghost not wanting to be around when Rondo got the news. Knowing all hell was gonna break loose. She knew Rondo was cutthroat and shit was going to get hot.

"Yo everybody get the fuck back." A kid named LA shouted. "If ya'll don't know anything get the hell outta here." LA ordered taking control of the situation. Then he pulled out his phone and dialed Rondos number.

As Rondo dialed King Charles number he received a call. He looked at the caller I.D. and seen it was one of his young wolves down in Clara Cox, immediately he answered figuring that he would call King Charles later. When he had more to tell him.

"Yo what up." Rondo answered.

"What's good big bruh this is L.A."

"I know who this is, what's going on?"

"We have a problem down here, somebody in a white van just came through and dumped Money-B's body on the street."

"You better not be playing wit me." Rondo hollered.

"I wouldn't dare play like that."

"Did anybody see who did or what happened?" Rondo asked.

"Everybody seen it."

"And nobody busted on them fools." Rondo said more of a statement than a question shaking his head.

"Shit happened so fast nobody have time to react." LA replied.

"Ok, look I'm in Charlotte right now, this what I want you to do, you listening?"

"Yeah."

"You got that reup money right?"

"Yeah I got sixteen thou."

"Listen up. First I want you to get the bosses body off the street. Take him to Westbrooke Funeral Home. Ask for Mike give him five bands and tell him I said to take care of that. Keep five bands for yourself and give that remaining 6 to BG and tell him to come see me at the Charlotte Mansion."

"Okay I'm on it."

"Hurry up and get the boss off the street before someone in the hood call the police. Call me back when everything is taken care of. I'll have something else for you youngin." Rondo finished and then hung up.

When Rondo hung the phone up he redialed King Charles number.

"Hello." King Charles answered on the first ring.

"How are you doing Mr. Charles, this is Rondo."

"My grandson's old friend right."

"Yes sir. I have some news I need to tell you."

"Go ahead body spit it out.

"Mikal is dead sir they threw his body out on the streets in Clara Cox. My wolves recovered the body he should be at Westbrooke Funeral Home in High Point."

"Dead you say? Them damn Santiago's threw my grandson out on the street like a dog. I will kill them all for this." King Charles hollered.

"I spoke with my great granddaughter. I'm glad she is safe. She told me about the exchange." King Charles said.

"Sir is there anything you can tell me so I can hunt his killers down?" Rondo asked.

"You leave Kanden to me. I will take care of him personally. You can find Justice in Chapel Hill. Kill him and bring me his head, if you fail me I will have your head in the place of his. Now you have a good day son, okay."

"Yes sir." Rondo answered and then he heard the dial tone.

Hanging the phone up with Rondo King Charles got up from his recliner chair and walked over to the wall intercom and hit the com button.

"Ra'mon, I need you to come up here for a second. I need to give you instruction."

"I'm coming up now sir."

"Thank you Ra'mon." King Charles replied as he walked back to his old recliner chair and sat down.

Within minutes Ra'mon came walking in. "Mr. Charles what is it you need me to do?" Ra'mon asked.

"My grandson has been killed Kanden won the war, but to add insult to injury he had Mikal's body thrown out on the street like a dog how dare he disrespect me. I want you to personally go to High Point and bring my grandson home. His body is at Westbrooke Funeral Home. Before you leave I want you to contact Rahman tell him it's time to come home. He already knows what his orders are."

"Everything will be taken care of you need not worry, have you taken all of your meds for today?" Ra'mon asked.

"No. Send the nurse up before you go, have her bring me some orange juice. I'm getting thirsty."

"Yes sir." Ra'mon replied turning to walk out the door.

"Ra'mon." King Charles said stopping his general in his tracks.

"Yes sir."

"Be gentle with my grandson."

"I will sir." Ra'mon replied as he turned and walked out the door.

When Ra'mon got downstairs he sent the nurse up with King Charles meds and a glass of freshly squeezed orange juice just the way the old man liked it. When that was taken care of only then did he walk outside the mansion and have one of his soldiers bring his S550 Benz around followed by a huge black Chevy travel van to carry Money-B's body inside. After getting inside his

Benz he pulled out his iPhone and texted Rahman

Text: It's time to come home brother.

Rahman's return text came quickly, as if he was waiting for orders. I will be home tonight Rahman texted back.

Ra'mon smiled to himself, as he looked at Rahman's text knowing no one was better at murder than his baby brother. Sitting his phone inside the car holder Ra'mon pulled off heading towards High Point North Carolina to bring King Charles' grandson home.

Justice was glad that everything had been taken care of and that no one in his family had been hurt. The first thing he did when he got back to Chapel Hill was pick Lisa up. He had still been driving Money-B's Lambo when he pulled up on Red Bull to get Lisa. When they both came out of the old house to meet him they both were surprised at the wheels he was driving. Justice had gotten out, and pulled Red Bull to the side giving him the full rundown before leaving with his girl. That had been two days ago. Now after coming in to his new found fortune. He was in no rush to put more guns or product on the streets, so he and Lisa went on a vacation to Miami Beach to get away from everything for a lil while.

"Baby I know you do some things that I don't really approve of, but you're my man. I wanta be in the game with you. I don't wanta be at home wondering if you're coming home or not. I want us to be like Bonnie and Clyde." Lisa said as they sat on the balcony in the hotel suite at the Hilton watching the water.

"Baby you know I love you, but we're not Bonnie and Clyde we're Justice and Lisa." Justice smiled.

"What is it exactly that you wanta do baby?" Justice asked putting his arm around Lisa's neck pulling her close and kissing her on the cheek.

"I don't know Justice. I just want to feel important."

"You're my other half you'll always be important to me."

"I know I just want something to do."

"Okay since you want something to do." Justice paused and took Lisa's hand in his. "Let's go down to the beach and rub our toes in the sand. I want us to just enjoy ourselves right now. We'll talk about everything else when we get back."

Lisa smiles, and rubbed the back of Justice hand. "Okay baby."

Chapter 12

Vengeance is Mine

As Kanden slept Rahman sat in the living room and drunk a cold glass of water. He thought about the text that he had gotten from his brother. He had grown to like Kanden, but his loyalty would always lie with King Charles for what he had done for him and his brother. When his mother and father were killed by a neighborhood street gang in Dade County King Charles had taken them both in, and raised him and his brother Ra'mon like his own sons. He had even raised Ra'mon to the status of general which was a surprise because he could have easily given that position to his grandson Mikal. Mikal was soft, and they all knew it, but still he was the only blood tie to King Charles. By that right Mikal deserved to be his general. Rather than choose Mikal he chose his brother Ra'mon for his relentless way of violence, and sent Mikal away to take over North Carolina. But the Santiago's always stood in the way of Mikal's success,

Rahman was trained and sent to infiltrate Kanden's ranks. When the time came he was to kill Kanden. As he sat on the couch he battled within himself between loyalty and love. The fact of the matter was he could not disappoint the man who had raised him, and turned him into the killing machine that he was. If he did he was sure that King Charles would kill his brother. Finishing up his glass of water Rahman sat the glass gently down on the table, then stood up, and walked upstairs heading to Kanden's room. He slowly turned the knob of the bedroom door and peeked inside before he entered. Seeing that Kanden was sound asleep he walked in pulled out his Glock, and point it at Kanden's head. Rahman thought about what he was about to do not wanting to shoot him. He tucked his Glock back inside his coat pocket, and reached down and picked up a pillow that laid next to Kanden's head. He took the pillow in both hands then press it over Kanden's face, Kanden kicked and squirmed as he suffocated trying his best to fight off death then his body became still as if he was a cemented statue. Rahman lifted the pillow and stared down at Kanden's still body his eyes were wide open, as if he was staring death in the face. For the last few days there had been no guards inside the Burlington mansion which was strange. It was as if he knew death was coming and he embraced it or he must have trusted him fully which Rahman doubted knowing that Kaden never trusted anybody. Feeling remorse he bent down and closed Kanden's eyes. "Rest easy." Rahman said, then he turned, and walked out. When he stepped outside he pulled out his phone and called King Charles.

'Ring' 'Ring'.

"Rahman." King Charles answered on the second ring.

"Father it is done." Rahman replied.

"Okay son come home, we have much to discuss."

"I'm on my way." Rahman replied, as he ended his call.

After getting careful instructions from King Charles he didn't wait for LA to call back. Rondo went ahead and put his plan in motion, calling LA back himself.

'Ring' 'Ring' 'Ring' 'Ring'

"Big bruh what's good?" LA Answered.

"Is everything taken care of?"

"Yeah, I've taken care everything with Money-B, I haven't hit BG up yet tho."

"Okay hit him after you get off the phone with me, this is what I want you to do. Give BG that six thousand, tell him I said to give you a couple bricks. I want you to go to Chapel Hill to move that work. In the process of doing that I want you to find out as much as you can about dude named Justice Santiago. After you find out what you can I want you to call me back."

"I got you big bruh. I'm bout to get on that now." LA Replied as he hung up with Rondo.

Hanging up, LA dialed BG's number.

"Yo." BG answered on the first ring.

"Bro, this is LA."

"What's up bro?"

"Money-B dead, his body was dumped in Clara Cox. I took care of it, and got his body off the street. I just got off the phone with Rondo he's in charge now. He told me to meet up with you and head to Chapel Hill. He wants me to find out some info on a guy name Justice Santiago."

"Yo, what the fuck you mean Money-B's dead?"

"He's gone man that's all I know."

"Aite scoop Trap up, and meet me at Short Stop."

"You're in Burlington?"

"Yeah."

"That's Kanden turf."

"I know that. I got a lil jump off over here, what do you need tho?"

"I need two bricks, then I'm headed to Chapel Hill. I'll bring Trap with me on this."

"Aite meet me at the Short Stop sto. I'll have the work with me."

"That's a bet, Rondo said call him A.S.A.P."

"Good look, I'll be at the sto, one hour don't be late."

"I'll be there." LA replied and then hung up. Pulling out of the parking lot of Westbrooke Funeral Home he headed to East Kivett Street to pick up Trap before going to meet BG.

The Next Day 10:30am

Agent Jacobe Slade slowly walked inside Kanden's mini mansion in Burlington. Scanning the area walking through the living room he noticed two Burlington cops writing in a notepad as they talked to a Mexican woman. Thinking she had to be someone of importance maybe a girlfriend or a lover, Agent Slade walked over and introduced himself.

"How are you doing officers? I'm Agent Slade F.B.I." He said flashing his badge.

"We're good, we're taking the statement of Mrs. Sanchez. She's the one that found the body and called 911." One of the officers replied.

"Officers do you mind if I ask her a couple of questions of my own. It won't take long."

"No by all means go ahead we can come back to her later. We have all of her information." One of the officers stated, as they walked off.

"I'm Agent Slade. Do you mind telling me exactly what you saw?"

"Huh, I work for Mr. Santiago. I'm the housekeeper. I came to work this morning as I do every day at 9:00am after I drop my children off with their grandmother. When I got here this morning the door was wide open. Which was strange because Mr. Santiago is always tough on security."

"Does he have body guards?" Agent Slade asked.

"Yes, he has two here at all times."

"Were they here when you came into the house?"

"No when I walked in, there was nobody here. I called for the body guards, but got no answer, so I walked up to Mr. Santiago's bedroom. The door was cracked, so I walked inside the check on him, being that he has cancer. He looked like he was sleeping. I didn't realize anything was wrong until I tried to wake him, so he could get ready for his cancer treatments." Mrs. Sanchez said.

"How many times a week was his treatment?"

"He's been getting really sick lately, so the doctors up'd his treatment to three times a week."

"Who takes him to his treatments?"

"His body guards of course."

"Can you tell me there names?"

"John John is the big dark skinned fella he has a big beard. I think he's Muslim or something. I caught him praying in the basement one time. I don't think Mr. Santiago knew tho. The other body guard is a light skinned fella with short hair and green eyes he's kinda skinny. I believe he knows Karate or something he used to train with Mr. Santiago before he got sick his name is Vinny."

"What did you do after you found out that Kanden Santiago was dead?"

"I called the police, and stayed on the phone until they got here, so I could let them inside."

"Okay Mrs. Sanchez, I have one more question."

"Ask away."

"Do you know anyone that might want to hurt Mr. Santiago?"

"No sir he had been talking about leaving the states, and going back to Japan. He had told all of his employees that his brother Justice Santiago would be taking over the family business."

"Justice you say."

"Yeah."

"Have you ever met him?"

"No sir nobody has."

"I don't have any more questions."

"Are you going to find out what happened to him?" Mrs. Sanchez asked beginning to cry.

"I will do the best I can. I promise you that." Agent Slade replied, as he shook her hand and began to walk upstairs.

When Agent Slade got upstairs he walked inside Kanden's room there were officers and medics all around. He pulled some latex gloves from his pocket and slapped them on so he wouldn't contaminate the crime scene. As he looked around he stumbled upon a picture of Vidah Santiago. He picked up the picture frame, and pulled the picture out when he did another picture fell out behind it. It was a picture of a young boy in his early twenties, he picked the picture up off the ground, and turned it over. The word Justice was written on the back realizing that everything was coming together now. He stuffed the two pictures inside his pocket it had been a long time, but it was time to go see Vidah. He wondered if she would even talk to him after having locked her daughter Danielle away. He had to try for Justice's sake. If Kanden was dead that meant King Charles was behind it somehow, and if that was the case he would be after Justice also. Agent Slade thought to himself, and he turned and walked out of Kanden's bedroom out the mansion and into his truck. Cranking it up Agent Slade pulled off headed to see Vidah Santiago. After a little over an hours drive he pulled into the driveway of Vidah's three bedroom home in Siler City. He slowly got out and walked towards the house, before he could knock Vidah Santiago slung the door open.

"How dare you come to my house?" Vidah said.

"Ma'am, I didn't come here for trouble." Agent Slade replied as he took off his hat.

"What do you want?"

"Your grandson Kanden is dead. The housekeeper found his early this morning. May I come inside so we can talk?"

Vidah sighed after hearing that Kanden was dead. "You are not welcome in my home Jacobe! I don't care what the circumstances are. I want you off my land now. I may not be the woman I use to be, but I'm not above feeding you to my hogs. I'm not sure the F.B.I. would miss you or let alone believe a old lady like myself killed the famous Jacobe Slade I should feed you to my pigs." Vidah Santiago threatened.

"I am still a federal agent Mrs. Santiago."

"That may be true, but you are a back stabbing pig to me. You locked my daughter away remember."

"She deserved it." Slade hollered.

"She didn't deserve shit, but your loyalty. I wonder what the F.B.I. would think if they found out you were sleeping with my daughter. You are a dirty cop Jacobe. You are not the hero the people think you are."

"Maybe not Mrs. Santiago, but I'm not here to talk about me. I'm here to talk about Justice. He's in trouble, if Kanden's dead that means King Charles must have killed him. He will be going after Justice next since he will be taking over the family business."

"Mind your tongue Jacobe, and stay out of family business. You may be a fed, but you are not above my family, and you know that." Vidah Santiago spat.

"You're right, I'm only here to help Justice. I know you don't want to lose another grandson to this family war."

"I will take care of my grandson. Thank you for stopping by and informing me about Kanden, but I have no more words for you." Vidah Santiago replied slamming the door in his face.

Vidah Santiago watched Agent Slade all the way until he pulled off, and was out of sight. Walking back to her den, she slowly sat back down on her couch and thought about what she had to do.

King Charles had broken the rules by involving himself in the beef between their grandsons. Now she had to put him to sleep. Vidah thought to herself as she reached under the couch and pulled out a small box. Looking inside she pulled out a medium size 9mm Taurus equipped with a silencer. She checked the clip and pulled the slider back then began taking the old gun apart. After taking it apart she cleaned it then put it back together. Walking to the window, she raised it up then pointed the 9mm outside at an old stop sign that had been nailed to a tree. She cocked the 9mm back then squeezed the trigger firing two rounds hitting the stop sign dead center. *I still got it.* She thought to herself then she shut the window, and picked up her phone and called Justice.

"Hey grandma." Justice answered picking up on the first ring.

"Hey baby, grandma needs you to come home right away. Your brother has been killed."

"What happened?"

"Can't talk over the phone. Come home now grandma needs you."

"Okay grandma, I'm coming me and Lisa will catch the first flight back to North Carolina."

"I love you Justice."

"I love you to grandma." Justice replied before hanging up.

Hanging the phone up Vidah put on some fresh clothes and left the house to see to her grandson's arrangements.

Chapter 13

Goons Don't Play

After meeting with BG, LA, and Trap headed to Chapel Hill. When they got there they checked into a hotel that wasn't too far from the U.N.C. campus, but close enough for them to move around. Immediately after checking in they left out, and hit a couple neighborhoods promoting the work they were selling and also asking about Justice Santiago. A couple days passed and the work gone, they were both in a celebrating mood as they popped bottles with two white girls satisfied about the information they gathered.

Outside Harlem World, Red Bull, and Halftime were waiting for the right time to kick the door down. The fact that the two out of towners room was secluded, all the way in the back they didn't worry about putting masks on, and hiding their faces. Red Bull checked his watch it was 12:30. Harlem World stood on the right side of the door while Halftime stood on the left. Red Bull was set to kick the door in with his size fifteen Timberland covered foot.

LA and his partner Trap were enjoying the sight, and sounds of Abby and Tiffany sixty-nining each other, when they were interrupted by the sudden crash from the door being kicked in. They didn't stand a chance the three gunmen were on them like flies on shit with their guns drawn.

"Everybody get the fuck on the floor. Face down ass up." Harlem World shouted.

"Especially you two." Halftime said admiring the two naked white girls.

"Let's not make this difficult, where's the bread?" Red Bull asked.

"What the fuck are you talking about?" LA said playing dumb right before Harlem World kicked him in the face causing blood to gush from his sunken nose.

"Argh." LA shouted in pain trying to cover his nose then Harlem World viciously kicked him in the ribs.

"Ain't nobody tell you to move." Harlem World shouted. Halftime bent down trying to reason with LA.

"You're making this shit harder than it needs to be." Halftime said.

"Yo hold this." Red Bull said handing his weapon to Halftime before grabbing a naked LA up by his head standing six foot five two hundred and seventy pounds Red Bull had no trouble throwing LA across the room landing with a thud.

"Urgh." LA grunted.

"Where's the loot and the work?" Halftime asked stepping over towards Trap.

"Everything is wrapped up in the bathroom inside the toilet." Trap answered not wanting to go through the shit LA just did.

Hearing that Harlem World shot to the bathroom and threw the toilet lid on the floor. "Bingo." Exclaimed Harlem World, as he reached inside, and pulled out of a trash bag. Looking inside he seen a lil work, and rolls of money. Satisfied with his findings he walked back in the room and joined his partners.

"I got one more question, and it would be smart if you answered it honestly." Harlem World stated eyeing each occupant to make sure he had everyone's attention.

"Why the fuck are you two asking questions about Justice Santiago?" Harlem asked.

"But before you answer with a lie… I want you show ya'll what my name is." Harlem stated taking his Glock, and shooting Abby in the knee cap.

"Aaaah." Abby shouted after her knee exploded from her leg.

"Now would ya'll like to answer my question?" Harlem World asked.

"Ya'll got 30 seconds and ten are already gone."

"On my mama. I'm just out here trying to get money man." LA stated in pain.

"That's not the answer I'm looking for." Harlem World stated right before popping Abby in her other knee cap, Abby fell to the floor, and passed out from pain.

"Oh my God please stop." Begged Tiffany as she rushed to her friend's side.

"Sweetie did I tell you to move?" Harlem World said as he hit her over the head with the butt of his Glock knocking her unconscious. "That's what you get for not following instructions."

"I-I-I was looking because Rondo paid me." A painful LA uttered.

"Why?" Red Bull shouted.

"Somebody dumped Money-B body in the street. Someone mentioned his name to Rondo."

"So Rondo knows who Justice is huh?" Harlem World asked really to himself.

"How are you and Rondo communicating?" Harlem asked.

"Man I told you all I could, my word yo." LA sweared.

"Ain't no way you worried about snitching now are you?" Harlem World asked the rhetorical questions.

"Fuck you." LA spat.

"Oh you wanta be tough now?" Harlem World asked comically looking at his partners.

"Go ahead and kill me that's all I'm telling you." LA taunted trying to get them to get this shit over wit he was tired of being tortured.

"Aite if that's what you want." Harlem World said as he raised his Glock and shot LA in the face. Instantly killing him. Then him and his partners left the same way that they came.

After he was sure that the intruders were gone, Trap left the room leaving LA's dead body, and the two unconscious girls alone. He needed to put some distant between himself and his current situation. Trap knew that Rondo wasn't going to like the message that Justice's crew had sent him, but he'd rather escape and live to see another day, than to lose his life in a motel room over some bullshit. He really didn't give two fucks about. Ultimately he had two things to take care of. First, he'd relay the message to Rondo by phone. No way was he putting his neck on the chopping block by pulling up personally, plus this would give himself time to put his second plan into motion. Which was hitting his stash spot and getting the fuck outta High Point. Getting lucky he found a ride and shot straight to his spot that he shared with his girl. When he got there he paid the driver and thanked him then he rushed to the front door.

"Oh my God baby, what happened?" Trap's girl asked with genuine concern while caressing his face.

"Nothing, you need to pack some clothes, where's your

phone?" Trap wanted to know.

"On the kitchen counter, and what do you mean packs some clothes?"

"Look Crystal! I don't have time to explain, shit's fixing to hit the fans." Trap answered with agitation in his voice.

"I'll be back." Trap said taking Crystal's phone with him as he walked outside and called Rondo.

'Ring' 'Ring' 'Ring'.

"Yo who dis?" Rondo answered.

"It's LA's homeboy Trap."

"Aite speak what's up."

Trap relayed the whole story from the time the duo left until the robbery, and murder of LA, to the two severely beaten girls, to his release. He also relayed the message that Justice's crew had sent.

"Where you at now fam?" Rondo asked.

"I'm on my way to the hood to lay low." Trap lied trying to buy himself some time not taking any chances.

"Come through the nitty gritty. I got something for you." Rondo invited.

"Nah I'm good. I'm just going to lay low get my face off the street for a while." Trap replied.

"You sure you don't need anything?" Rondo asked.

"No big bruh I'm good." Trap said trying to end the conversation.

"Get at me if you need me tho." Trap offered the fake sentiment.

"I'll hit you later." Rondo stated trying to figure out the best course of action before deciding to go full steam ahead his plan came together as he decided to infiltrate Justice's crew feeling he had to find a way in. He picked up the phone and called Danger.

Justice and Lisa had returned from their Miami vacation. His grandmother had already set up the funeral arrangements for his brother's funeral which was a blessing because he didn't know where to start at when it came to stuff like that. As soon as he had gotten off the plane he had received a call from Harlem World letting him know that some guys had come to Chapel Hill looking for him. Harlem World had assured him that it had been taken care of, but his mind still wondered. Pushing his thoughts of the violence to come away he sat down with his grandmother.

"Grandma why didn't you tell me the truth?" Justice asked.

"I did tell you the truth baby, I just didn't tell you all of it."

"Why not?"

"Because you weren't ready yet. I needed to be sure and so did Kanden."

"Ready for what grandma?"

"To take over, as the family head in the south."

"Why don't you tell me everything from the top. Now that Kanden's dead. I don't want to go into the family business blind."

"Okay! It all started with your grandfather Raymond and my sister's ex-husband Charles Sanderson. He goes by the name of King Charles you may have heard of him."

"I have." Justice confirmed.

"Well your grandfather and Charles started beefing over 100 kilos of pure Columbian cocaine that came up missing. Come to find out Charles brother Hector hijacked the shipment and sold the work to their rival, the Mexican cartel. Raymond was furious, and wanted Charles to kill his brother Hector for his disloyalty of course he refused. Charles refusal didn't sit well with your grandfather, so he had Charles brother kidnapped, and killed then sent Hector's dead body to the Mexicans cut up and stuffed inside a oil barrel. The Mexicans informed Charles of the news. Charles was hurt, as he should have been but nobody thought he would join forces with the Mexican cartel, but he did. Charles and the Cartel waged war on your grandfather. A lot of people died during that time more on Charles side than Raymond's. We had help, we have a strong family up north in Manhattan New York, they assisted your grandfather." Vidah sighed before she continued. "My sister Destiny took Charles side against her own family. She was his wife and she was pregnant. The beef went on for years well after Destiny had her baby. It went on until a hit Charles had sent took Raymond's life. Raymond saved me that day. He gave his life for mine by covering me as our limo was rippled with bullets."

"So what happened after that?"

"I avenged your grandfather by taking control of the family. I sent your mother up north so she would be safe, as I wreaked havoc on Charles family. I had everyone killed but Charles. I wanted him to live and suffer as I destroyed every member of the Sanderson family."

"What happened to your sister?"

"I let her live and suffer. Your mother killed her, when I retired, my sisters daughter Janet was raised by Charles. When she came of age she gave birth to a son name Mikal. Six months later Janet was killed in a drive by shooting between rival gang in Atlanta. Charles raised Mikal like his own son."

"So the man I killed was my cousin?"

"Yes, but do not feel pain for him. He would have killed you if given the chance."

"I am killing family grandma this is sick."

"They are not family. I am your family, your sister is your family, Amir is your family. The person you killed was the blood of a traitor."

"But Kanden is dead, how could that happen?"

"Charles interfered. He broke the rules for Mikal."

"So it was King Charles that had him killed?"

"Yes he is the only one who could have touched Kanden. None of Mikal's soldiers had that kind of reach that could touch someone like your brother."

"So what do I do grandma?"

"You finish it, I'll take care of Charles you won't need to worry about him."

"How do you expect to do that?"

"I have my ways Justices, even tho I am a old woman now, I still have the power of our family behind me."

"You know what grandma?"

"What is it?"

"I can't believe that my grandma used to be in the streets."

"We all have our past Justice, we all come from somewhere, know this." Vidah paused as she placed her hands on Justices shoulder. "You have the power now be mindful of how you use it. The streets are always watching. Never break your covenant and always stay true to your word understand."

"Yeah, my brother knew he would die, he told me I had to bury him."

"Yes he did, and now we will bury him. We will prepare for his funeral. The family heads will be down to pay their respects. I will introduce you to them. Always remain respected and loyal and listen when they speak. If ever there is a situation they will come to your aid."

"The funeral will be held two days from now."

"Okay grandma." Justice replied as he stood up getting ready to leave.

"Who is dis?" Justice asked as he reached for the torn paper his grandmother handed him.

"His name is Monte Santiago. He is your cousin, and also the family accountant. He will let you know of all the business you now own, and the stocks, and shares you now hold. He is already waiting for your call. Call him when you are relaxed."

"Okay grandma I'll call him, how's Zeenah doing?"

"She good she's at practice right now. She be home in about a hour. If you want to wait."

"No I have to get going, you've given me a lot to process. I need a lil time to think." Justice replied as he hugged his grandmother.

"I love you baby, and I want you to be careful out there."

"I love you too and I will grandma I promise."

"Okay baby I'ma hold you to that." Vidah replied as she watched her grandson leave headed to his truck.

Chapter 14

Warning Signs and Roots

"All rise." The bailiff bellowed. "The honorable Judge Jason Squires presiding." The bailiff finished.

"You may be seated." Judge Squires stated while shuffling papers.

"The state of North Carolina versus Justice Santiago on multiple charges of murder, extortion, drug trafficking, kidnapping, and racketeering." District Attorney Brandon Timberlake said while he stood up in his Ralph Lauren three piece suit. Strolling confidently towards the jury box. He leaned over, and began his opening argument.

"Ladies, and gentlemen of the jury. I will prove without a shadow of a doubt that the defendant sitting here today is guilty of every charge on this docket." D.A. Timberlake stated while staring each juror in the eyes.

"Justice Santiago is the mastermind and the head of the biggest criminal enterprise North Carolina has ever seen. The Santiago Crime Family. Over the next few days you will hear numerous testimonies, and see exhibits that seem like they were straight out of movie or television show. I assure each and every one of you that all these atrocious acts are very real, and if he is not found guilty Justice Santiago will continue to run his crime syndicate, and his crimes will only become bolder and more vicious." D.A. Timberlake paused for a dramatic effect.

"You will also hear testimonies that will paint the defendant as a pillar of the community. I urge every one of you not to look thru smoke tinted glasses. Don't be fooled by the baby faces looks. This man here is a cold blooded killer." D.A. Timberlake said as he power walked to the defendants table before continuing. "You will be presented with clear evidence that will prove that this case is cut and dry. Once you hear all of the evidence you should all come to the unanimous decision that Justice Santiago is guilty." The D.A. said while straightening his tie as he walked back to his table where his assistant handed him a chrome forty-five.

"This man should be sentenced to death." The D.A. said as he raised the chrome forty five and pulled the trigger. 'Bloc.'

Justice instantly woke up with a jolt wiping sweat from his face.

"Baby what's wrong?" A startled Lisa asked.

"Nothing baby, just a bad dream go back to sleep." Justice replied as he assured her he was okay after Lisa laid back down. He checked his watch it was 10:30 am. Grabbing his phone off the table he speed dialed Amir's number.

"Yo what up?" Amir groggily answered half way sleep himself.

"Get dressed we're going to South Carolina." Justice replied.

"This early man, for what?"

"I need to see Jenny, so get dressed. I'll be there in a few."

"Aight man damn. I'm getting up now." Amir replied as he hung up the phone.

Following his call with Amir, Justice got out of bed and got dressed grabbed his keys and his baby .380 and hit the door headed to the Dirt Road to pick Amir up.

As soon as he grabbed Amir they headed to South Carolina. After the two and a half hour drive from Chapel Hill. They were pulling into the big gravel drive way and following it until they came to a ramshackle two story house.

Justice and Amir waited until they were told they could get out the car and enter into the house. Accompanied by an older man that looked as if he was sixty years old or older.

"Have a seat." The old man said as he pointed to the only couch in the living room. "Jenny will be with you in a moment." The old man stated before leaving and disappearing into the back.

"Damn, he could've offered us something to drink at least." Amir said.

"Shut the fuck up retarded ass." Justice replied while snickering stopping his giggles as the old man returned to the living room.

"Jenny will see you now." The old man stated while pointing at Justice.

"Wait, how the fuck does she know that I'm the one that came to see her?"

"Jenny knows, and see's all Justice." The old man said revealing that he knew his name sent chills through Justice body.

Feeling weirded out, he followed the old man through the house into the kitchen, and out onto the back deck that was enclosed in a mosquito net. The two came to a stop at a well-worn kitchen table.

"You can stop staring and have a seat young man." Jenny ordered before finishing. "And tell me your problems."

"I thought you saw and knew all." Justice tested smartly.

"Hmph." She grunted.

"I know that you've been having bad dreams, and from your aura you've done a lot of bad things." Jenny said. "Now do you want to tell me what's going on, and what you need?" Jenny asked.

Closing his eye Justice shuddered and began telling Jenny his dreams and about the promises that he had made to himself as well as everything he felt she needed to know. After Jenny listened to every word that Justice had to say she got up, and walked inside the house leaving Justice by himself. He could hear the old woman rummaging in the kitchen. After she found what she was looking for she walked out onto the net covered deck.

"Come with me." Jenny demanded leading Justice inside a wooden shed. When they entered there were different herbs, oils, spices, and various animal parts sitting on shelves. Jenny collected her ingredients and went to her work station and began mixing the ingredients into a pewter bowl letting that sit, she started mixing the dry ingredients, and placed them into a small velvet like bag. Closing her eyes she began to chant in prayer. Justice got goosebumps from watching the old woman sway side to side. Justice thought he was tripping when he started seeing the bag smoke without having any heat applied to it. When Jenny had finished her chant she turned to Justice.

"Do you believe in a higher power or spirits that can harm or protect you?" Jenny asked.

"Yes." Justice answered.

"You've got evil spirits surrounding you. The reason they haven't been able to get to you is because people are praying for the safety of your soul. Whatever you are trying to accomplish there are people hoping you fail. You came to me in the nick of time the spirits were getting closer. Here drink this." Jenny ordered handing Justice her liquid mix, he slowly reached for it then drunk it.

"Good, that will cleanse the evil from you and this." Jenny said, as she handed Justice a small black bag. "This will protect you. Keep it on you at all times best in your wallet or inside your shoes. Under no circumstances should anybody else touch it. If they do the protection will fade." Jenny explained.

"The bag protects your spirit not your physical." Jenny said as she looked at Justice making sure that he understood. When he nodded she gave her final instructions.

"Be sure to find a church or ask your higher power to protect you. You are about to come into a lot of money. A close friend of yours will betray you. What I have done is all I can do for you. What I've told you is all I can say the spirits will only let me see but so much. Please leave the money with Willie."

"I will, and thank you Mrs. Jenny." Justice replied before he walked out of the net deck, and back inside the house. When he walked in Amir was still sitting on the couch drinking a glass of water. Willie was posted up leaning on the wall. Justice walked over to him.

"How much? Jenny told me to pay you."

"Fifteen hundred." The old man answered.

"Damn bruh, what the hell you get?" Amir uttered.

"Nothing she told me what I needed to hear." Justice answered, as he reached inside his pocket and pulled from his wad fifteen crisp hundred dollar bills folded them, and stuffed them inside his pocket.

"Mrs. Jenny thanks you for your business, and please be mindful of whatever she told you."

"I will old man." Justice replied, as he headed to the door. "Come on Amir let's go." Then they both walked out and got inside Justice's Benz, and left bumping the old Reasonable Doubt album. As they made the two and a half hour drive back to Chapel Hill a lot of things ran through Justice's head. Jenny had said that someone close would betray him. He couldn't help wondering who it would be, as he looked over at Amir who had fallen asleep. Returning his eyes back to the road. Amir would never betray him they had been friends since they were in the sandbox playing with metal Tonka Trucks. Justice thought to himself. He would have to keep a close eye on everyone from now on. Finally when they got back to Chapel Hill it was six o'clock in the afternoon. He dropped Amir off the headed back home to see Lisa.

Pulling up in the driveway and walking back inside the house Lisa sat in the living room in her boy shorts. Justice walked over to her.

"Hey baby." Justice said as he bent down and kissed her on her soft lips.

"Hey honey, is everything okay? You look real tense."

"Yeah I'm fine just have a few things on my mind is all." Justice replied as he walked to their bedroom, and laid on the bed exhausted from the drive. A few minutes later Lisa appeared in the doorway looking sexy in her boy shorts. She seductively walked over to Justice then crawled on the bed, and laid beside her man. Justice put his arm around her and kissed her on the forehead.

"I love you Lisa, you know that right?"

"Yes baby I know." Lisa replied, as she stuck her hand in Justice pants and began playing with his dick.

"Baby what you doing?"

"You're all tense. I want to help you relieve your stress." Lisa answered as she began to unbutton Justices jeans then she pulled his dick out of it's confinement. She slowly stroked it a few times then she bent down and began slowly sucking him off, as if she was licking a lollipop trying to savor the flavor. When she knew that he was fully hard she removed her boy shorts her gold patch shining like a leprechauns treasure, then she slowly removed her shirt and bra. Justice kicked his shoes off, then Lisa slid his pants, and boxers off. Not wanting Justice to move Lisa crawled back on the bed putting Justices dick back in her mouth sucking him slowly, as she rubbed his stomach and chest. Not wanting him to come quickly, she stopped and got up. Justice tried to grab her but she swatted his hands away. She turned around with her butt facing him in reverse cowgirl position. She bounced her pussy up and down the shaft of Justices penis.

"Aah aaaah." Lisa moaned in pleasure taking all of her man in her.

Justice grabbed hold of Lisa's butt, and began to massage her butt cheeks, as she continued to bounce up and down.

"Damn Lisa I'm cuming." Justice said shooting his load deep. Lisa continued to bounce until she also came. "Aaaaah." Lisa moaned as Justice grabbed her by the hips as she made it rain on his dick. When he was sure she was finish he pulled out and Lisa laid beside him they both cuddled with each other until Lisa fell asleep. When Justice got up Lisa was still asleep feeling that this was the right time he pulled his pants back on and walked outside to the backyard and into his shed to retrieve a bag of dog food. He called to his pit bull Diamond and watched as she came running to her bowl. Sitting on all fours Diamond watched Justice pour her food. When he finish she raised her paw for Justice to shake it. After he did she dug in her bowl. Justice tied the bag back up then went and put it back to the place he had gotten it from. He continued to watch Diamond eat then pulled out his cell phone and called his cousin Monte Santiago the family accountant.

'Ring' 'Ring'.

"Hello Justice." Monte answered.

"What's good man?"

"I have been waiting on your call."

"Sorry it took me a lil while. I had a few things I needed to sort out."

"That's totally understandable given the current situation. Okay let's get down to business. You are now the head of Santiago Enterprises, congratulations."

"Thanks."

"I got your address from your grandmother Vidah. I mailed you a copy of all your assets it should be in your mail box now. Walk to it, and check it for me please."

"Okay I'm walking now." Justice replied, as he walked to the front yard and checked his mailbox. He opened it and pulled out a big brown envelope then he opened it up.

"I got it I'm looking at it now."

"Okay don't read it over the phone. Look at the papers sign them then return them back to me for review, and filing purposes. My address is on the last page in that envelope."

"I see it."

"Once everything is signed. Mail it right back."

"I got you on that."

"Kanden's funeral will be held tomorrow. The Manhattan family will be coming down to pay their respects. The heads will be expecting to see you, will that be a problem?"

"No, I will be there."

"Good, your grandmother Vidah speaks very highly of you. She is certain that you can hold your position. Even tho the elders are not all in agreement."

"The elders do not know me." Justice spat.

"You are young, some think you are too young to hold this position, but you are a Santiago by blood so there's no choice in the matter. Just know that they will destroy you, and replace you if you weaken them."

"I've never been weak in my life. I live on the edge. It's all or nothing for me. The streets raised me partner."

"As the family head you must always think like a business man, and never like some street thug. You are a multimillionaire now. Your every move will be watched. With great power comes great responsibilities."

"You talk to me about the elders. After speaking with me what do you think?"

"Justice, I'm just the family accountant, it doesn't matter what I think. When you die, if I'm still living, I will transfer funds and manage your successor, as I am doing you now that is my only job."

"Sounds boring, but to be able to do all that you must be smart?"

"I have a bachelor's degree from Harvard University in business management and a law degree from Yale. I guess you could say I'm pretty smart." Monte chuckled.

"I'm glad someone with brains will be looking over my money because honestly I don't know what the hell I'm doing right now."

"Don't worry Kanden didn't either at first. He kinda grew into it. I can say this Vidah has put everything on the line for you don't let her down."

"I wouldn't dare."

"Okay then I'll see you tomorrow at the funeral don't forget to sign those papers, and mail that envelope back to me as soon as possible."

"I got you. I'm about to go inside, and get on that now." Justice replied and then hung the phone up and walked back inside.

Chapter 15

Married to the Family

Friday afternoon 1:30 pm family members and friends of Kanden Santiago assembled inside Deliverance Fellowship Church. The place was packed to capacity. Vidah Santiago, Justice, Zeenah, and the up north family took up the first ten rows. Dressed in all black they watched, as Kanden layed still inside his gold casket. Also dressed in black Armani suits were the five heads of the family. They listened as the pastor gave his sermon of the home coming of Kanden Santiago. His legacy was solidified, and would certainly be hard to follow Justice thought to himself, as he held Lisa's hand. When the pastor finished his sermon. It was time to view the body, and pay their last respects. The five Santiago heads stood up with roses in their hands. They all watched as Vidah Santiago paid her last respects to her grandson she hugged her granddaughter as she mourned Kanden, then she placed a rose inside his Armani suit over his heart. When she bent down, and placed the rose she whispered in Kanden's ear. "I know life was hard for you my grandson, but you are free now. You are in a better place. You have made your grandmother proud. On my life Charles will pay for this. I love you Kanden." Vidah Santiago finished as she patted Kanden's chest, shedding her tears, she walked away with her granddaughter in her arms.

The five heads including Justice came up all at once to pay their respects. Each one placed a rose inside the casket. An older man placed his rose in Kanden's hand then slid a single diamond ring on his finger. "Rest easy nephew." The older man whispered Justice looked around and noticed that the four people up front with him all wore the same ring. Then he himself patted Kanden's chest. "I will make you proud brother. I will earn their respect and avenge you." Justice whispered then he took a step back and stood beside the old man who had placed the ring on Kanden's finger. He watched as the other two members said their last words. When they were done each of the five members motioned to their generals to come to the front.

Justice motioned to Amir, and he followed the other four generals. All five generals walked up and stood beside the golden casket. As the five heads of the Santiago crime family walked away, and joined Vidah, and Zeenah outside. The rest of the family viewed the body, and then Kanden's friends and associates. After everyone gathered outside only then did the five generals lift the casket on their shoulders, then slowly walked their brother to his final resting places. Everyone watched as Kanden's casket was lowered into the ground. Vidah was the first to throw dirt on the casket followed by Justice, Lisa, Zeenah, and the four other family heads. After Kanden was laid to rest everyone in attendance began to disperse. As Justice stood with Lisa, he felt his grandmother tap him on the shoulder signaling for him to follow her. Together they walked to the other four family heads, and Vidah began to introduce her grandson to the powers that be.

"Justice this here is Manuel, he is the family head in New Jersey." Vidah said introducing the first member closest to her.

"How are you doing kid?" Manuel Santiago said, as he stuck out his hand.

"I'm fine nice to meet you." Justice replied shaking Manuel's hand.

Then Vidah moved on.

"This man here is Husain Razaq Santiago he is the family head in Philly."

"Assalamu Alaikum." Husain greeted.

"Wa Alaikum Assalam." Justice replied noticing the shock on Husain's face when he returned the greeting. "My general Amir is Muslim." Justice said.

"I like you already." Husain replied smiling to himself. Vidah moved on. "This man here is Pedro he is the family head in D.C."

"Nice to meet you Justice, and sorry for your loss." Pedro said.

"Nice to meet you too."

Vidah then moved on.

"Last and the most important Justice this here is Arturo Santiago Jefe de Jefe. In English we say the boss of all bosses." Vidah explained then she hugged Arturo. Justice noticed that Arturo was the old man that slid the diamond ring on Kanden's finger.

"It is nice to meet you sir." Justice said.

"It is good to finally meet you. You look just like your mother. I wonder are you as ruthless." Arturo said.

"I am sir, I took care of Kanden's rival."

"That you did, but Danielle would've chopped him up and sent him back to Charles one limb at a time. She was always my favorite, she was very thorough just like your grandmother." Arturo said. Vidah just looked at him and smiled. "Vidah we would like to speak to the boy alone. We have much to discuss with him." Arturo said. Vidah nodded and walked away and joined Monte as he continued to stand and stare at Kanden's casket as the grave diggers filled the hole. Arturo and the other three bosses took a few steps closer to Justice then Arturo reached inside his pocket and pulled out a small jewelry box and handed it to Justice. Justice opened it and his eyes lit up as he seen the diamond encrusted ring that had the name Santiago written in the setting lined with diamonds.

"Put that ring on your right hand. You are the Santiago south boss everything south belongs to you. You are married to the family now. Your mother was very dear to me Justice if you have any problems you call me, and I will loan you Rambo my head hitman. He is relentless when it comes to violence. My comrades are not sure that you can hold this position. But I know you have learned from your mother and you have my upmost confidence do not disappoint." Arturo said.

"I've never been a disappointment on my word I will handle things here. I just need you to give me the chance to fill these huge shoes. Tell me Arturo how long have you known my mother." Justice asked.

"When my brother Raymond was murdered your grandmother sent your mother to me. I raised her while your grandmother destroyed Charles family. I protected your mother for years. She was like a daughter to me." Arturo answered.

"I hear you talk about Charles."

"Do not ask me of him your grandmother will finish him soon. That is her task to complete."

"We are all here for you if needed." Husain said placing his hand on Justices shoulder.

"But I must go now, my wives hate to be kept waiting." Husain stated as he hugged each family head then headed to his blackout limo. After he walked away Pedro and Manuel followed suit. Only Arturo remained they both walked over to Vidah and Monte. They all spoke briefly before leaving Kanden behind.

Walking into the lobby of the Orange County Police Department followed by her mother. Tiffany Dixon was visibly nervous as she walked up to the intercom and pressed the button getting the attention of the desk sergeant.

"Umm I'm a witness to a murder." Tiffany said.

"Hold on a sec, let me see if I can find someone for you." The desk sergeant replied moments later Federal Agent Jacobe Slade appeared sticking his hand out.

"Hello Mrs. Dixon. I'm Agent Jacobe Slade, how may I help you?"

"I witnessed a murder that happened a couple of days ago near the UNC campus."

"Okay follow me so we can talk in a more secure area." Agent Slade replied as he led the way to a vacant office. "Would you like something to drink?"

"Water would be fine." Tiffany answered.

Agent Slade disappeared, and then came back with two bottles of water from the refreshment room.

"Now you say you witnessed a murder?" Agent Slade asked placing a small tape recorder on the desk. "Where would you like to begin?"

"Me and my friend Abby hooked up with two guys that called themselves LA and Trap." Tiffany closed her eyes, as she began telling the nightmare that she narrowly escaped. Agent Slade listened until the young girl finished her story, then he left for a couple of minutes and came back with a file. He flipped through it and noticed that Tiffany's name wasn't included in the file. So she wouldn't have been part of the preliminary investigation.

"Your friend was shot in both knee caps am I right?"

"Yes."

"Then why did you leave?"

"I left because I was afraid."

"Why didn't you come forward with this information earlier?"

"I was terrified and I thought I'd be a target, I couldn't sleep without telling someone."

"You said LA and Trap were out of towners, do you know where they were from or why they came to Chapel Hill?" Agent Slade asked.

"I don't know where they were from all I know is they had

a lot of money and they were asking around about a guy name Justice Santiago. I think the guys that murdered LA were friends of Justice."

Agent Slade eyes lit up when she said Justice name.

"Can you describe the guys that kicked the door in, you said they weren't wearing masks?"

"Yes, I can never forget them." Tiffany answered closing her eyes once more as she began painting a portrait of the three murderers.

Agent Slade turned around and grabbed a metal binder off the desk and opened it up. It contained various photos and mug shots. Pulling the metal clamps open Agent Slade removed six photos and sat them on the table in front of Tiffany. When she recognized one of the perps she literally jumped out of her chair. As her mother tried to calm her down. Agent Slade looked down at the picture.

"Bingo I got cha you son of a bitch." Agent Slade whispered to himself. "Mrs. Dixon you may be called to testify as the states witness and maybe a federal witness. I am offering you witness protection." Agent Slade said as he placed a piece of paper in front of Tiffany. "This here Mrs. Dixon is a statement saying you have been informed of your rights as a witness please sign where the three x's are marked. Agent Slade instructed as he watched Tiffany sign the paper.

"Thank you Mrs. Dixon. The information you provided is greatly valuable and appreciated." Agent Slade said and then left to find a uniformed officer to escort them both to witness protection. After finding an officer Agent Slade put out an A.P.B. for a black male mid-twenties, 5' 10 light skin with corn rows. His name is Deion Harper he goes by the name Halftime he is wanted for murder and is considered armed and dangerous approach with extreme caution.

10:30pm the same day as Kanden's funeral. Rondo sat at the sports bar taking heavy shots as he watched the Golden State and Chicago Bulls game. The game wasn't of any importance everybody already knew who would win. He just enjoyed watching Stephen Curry knock three pointers down from damn near half court defying odds which is what he had to do. He felt like the walls were closing in now that King Charles sent a clear message by putting Kanden Santiago to sleep. It was his time now and he was definitely going to send the grim reaper. Calling for another shot Danger walked thru the door.

"Damn what took you so long?" Rondo asked and Danger sat down across form him in the booth.

"You wanted me to come all the way up here to Charlotte. When you could've met me closer. I don't speed unless it's time for someone to die." Danger spat.

"What have you found out for me?"

"I have a source inside the Chapel Hill Police Department, a witness came thru and identified one of the murder suspects his name is Deion Harper but goes by the name Halftime. I'm pretty sure he's connected to Justice. If you can get to him before the cops get him he may be able to lead you to the man you want."

"What do you mean by that? I need you to handle this shit." Rondo spat. "Take that info you got from your connect start there and work your way up."

"No that's where you start." Danger shot back.

"Well what the fuck am I paying you for?"

"First off you ain't paying me shit, Money-B was." Danger spat while reaching into the waistband of his slacks with lightning speed revealing his two chrome .357's pointing them at Rondos head. "Money-B gone now. I'm a free agent, I hope I don't have to explain that to you in detail. And before your goons pull out those forty-fives. I'd advise you to assess the situation. Check your tone, and pay like you weigh. If you want my services." Danger demanded with venom in his voice.

"Whoa, whoa easy man let's not jump the gun here, my bad

fam." Rondo said while throwing a twenty five thousand dollar filled manila envelope on the table trying not to get shot. "Just do what you do take care of it how you see fit. Just get it done. I'll have the rest of the money tomorrow."

"See that you do." Danger voiced as he tucked his three fifty sevens, got up from the booth and headed out the door.

Rondo called for another shot, as he watched Danger slowly walk out of the bar then he pulled out his phone and called an old female friend of his name Maleekah. On the third ring Maleekah picked up. "Hello." Maleekah said in her sexy voice.

"What's up man?" Rondo asked smoothly.

"Nothing, what's good daddy?" Maleekah asked.

"That's what's up look I got a job for you."

"Okay anything for you boo."

"I'm at the Star Bar come see me."

"I'm on the way baby." Maleekah said and then hung up.

Rondo sat his phone down then swigged his shot as he waited on Maleekah. Forty-five minutes later walking through the double doors of the Star Bar. Maleekah knew all eyes were on her. She simply glowed standing at five foot six weighing one forty dudes broke their necks trying to catch a glimpse of the brown eye caramel goddess. As she strolled a few even got slapped by their significant other as they were caught in the act.

"I should've known you were in the bar when shit got quiet, damn ma." Rondo exclaimed after eyeing the tan Gucci cat suit looking like it was glued to her luscious frame.

"Boy stop." Maleekah shot back modestly.

"Nah, for real tho, I need something done and only you can do it."

"Shit! You know I'm about my bread what's the job?"

"I need you to go to Chapel Hill and try to get close to this guy Justice Santiago or his homie Amir. Work your magic and report to me on a weekly basis. They stay posting shit on Facebook so that's how you'll find out what they look like." Rondo stated.

"Okay you know my fee." Maleekah replied.

"You know I got cha." Rondo confirmed as he got up from his booth.

"I'm sorry to hear about Money-B. I know that was your man."

"It's okay no worries." Rondo replied then he walked out the bar with his goons in tow. Maleekah headed back home to begin getting ready for her new mission. When she got home the first thing she did was grab her beloved Grey Goose vodka. Putting Chris Brown on in her stereo she pulled out her laptop and logged into her Facebook page. She began to surf until she found Justice's page. Studying the multiple pictures and post, Maleekah noticed that Justice made numerous post about his girlfriend Lisa O'Neal. Clicking on Lisa's page she studied her bio making note that she worked at Richard Murray & Associates which was a small law firm in Chapel Hill. Seeing this Maleekah decided that the angle she would take would be through Lisa instead of going through Justice or any of his friends guys could be more guarded than females. She made a mental note to call Richard Murray and Associate's in the morning being that she had nothing else to do, she logged out of her Facebook page and began checking Chapel Hill's local posting for something decent. Not caring about the price knowing that Rondo would give her every dime she spent back and more. After finding what she wanted she logged off her computer and went upstairs. Running herself a nice bubble bath Maleekah undressed and climbed inside picking up her nine-inch dildo that she affectionately nicknamed Tom she placed the tip at the moist opening of her soaking wet pussy closing her eyes letting the liquor, music, and bubble bath take her where she needed to go. Inserting Tom Maleekah moaned, as she slid the dildo in and out of her wet throbbing pussy. After she climaxed, she drifted off to sleep.

Chapter 16

Devil's Motivation

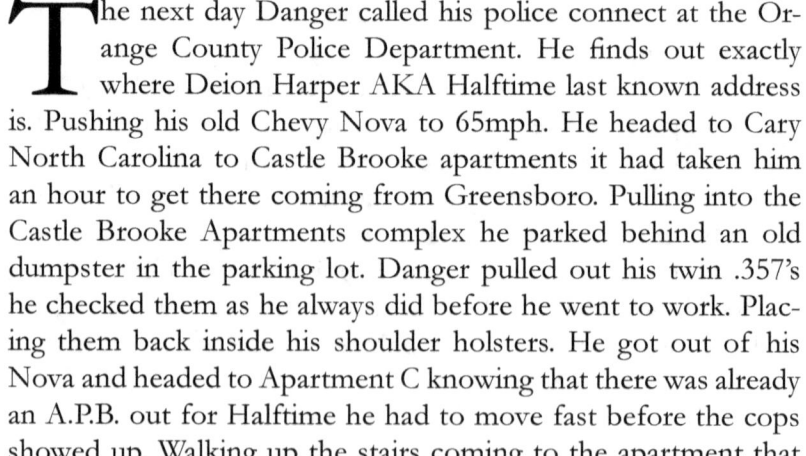

The next day Danger called his police connect at the Orange County Police Department. He finds out exactly where Deion Harper AKA Halftime last known address is. Pushing his old Chevy Nova to 65mph. He headed to Cary North Carolina to Castle Brooke apartments it had taken him an hour to get there coming from Greensboro. Pulling into the Castle Brooke Apartments complex he parked behind an old dumpster in the parking lot. Danger pulled out his twin .357's he checked them as he always did before he went to work. Placing them back inside his shoulder holsters. He got out of his Nova and headed to Apartment C knowing that there was already an A.P.B. out for Halftime he had to move fast before the cops showed up. Walking up the stairs coming to the apartment that he was looking for he knocked on the door. 'Knock', 'Knock'.

"Who is it?" A female voice hollered.

Danger didn't say a word he just kept knocking.

"Hold on, damn I'm coming." The girl said, as she slung the door open.

As soon as the door came open Danger kicked the Asian girl in the chest instantly dropping her to the ground. Danger pulled one of his .357 from his shoulder holster and pointed at the Asian girl as he walked closer to her putting a finger to his lips indicating for her to be quiet. Instead the girl screamed. Danger then grabbed the girl by her hair, and dragged her farther inside, as he shut the door behind him. "Where the fuck is Halftime pretty one?" Danger spat, then smiled as he used the barrel of his .357 and traced the poor girl's body from the breast down to her pussy. "I don't want to have to hurt you, but I will if you don't tell me what I wanta know. I never had a shot of Asian pussy before." Danger said kissing the girl on the cheek.

"Please don't hurt me, the money and the drugs are under the bed in a suitcase you can have it take it all please just don't hurt me." The Asian girl cried.

"I don't want money and drugs."

"Then what do you want, please don't rape me. My man will be back soon." She said trying to scare Danger. Danger smiled at what the pretty lil Asian girl said. "What is your name?" Danger asked.

"My name is Jazmine." She said, as fear made her voice tremble.

"Your man's name is Halftime?"

"Yes, and he'll be here soon."

"How soon?" Danger asked cocking the hammer back.

"He just went to the store to get some milk."

"Good, take your shoes off and hand them to me, then I want you to take the rest of your clothes off." Danger demanded.

Jazmine complied with Danger's orders she had taken clothes off until she had nothing on but her bra and panties, Danger snatched the shoe strings out of her shoes, and held them loosely in his hand.

"Take your bra and panties off too. I want you completely naked."

"Please, please don't make me do this please." Jazmine begged.

"Take your clothes off or die your choice it doesn't matter to me."

Afraid Jazmine unfastened her bra and rolled her panties down to her ankles and slid them off. Danger walked up to her grabbing her wrist Jazmine flinched in terror not knowing what to expect.

"I'm not going to rape you, if that's what you think, so calm down." Danger said, as he tied her wrist together and then her ankles. When she was secured he placed his cannon back in it's confinement. He picked Jazmine up and threw her over his shoulder then threw her on the couch.

"Don't move." Was all Danger said, as he disappeared into her bedroom and returned with a suitcase filled with money and cocaine he sat the case on the table and opened it up.

Eyeing the contents Danger smiled to himself. He hadn't come for this, but he would definitely take it as a bonus Danger thought to himself. Briefly getting up he snatched Jazmine's panties off the floor he brought them close to his nose and smelled them.

"Smells like grapes." Danger said walking up to Jazmine he ripped her panties and tied them around her mouth.

"Now be quiet it's time to wait on your boyfriend." Danger said cutting all the lights out then sat down on the couch next to Jazmine, and pulled out his hammer and waited.

Halftime pulled his Tahoe into the parking lot of Castle Brooke Apartments. Parking his truck he got out, and grabbed his groceries out the back of his truck, then he headed upstairs thinking about the wild sex he was going to have with Jazmine tonight. When he got to the door he fumbled with his keys until he found the right one. Sticking the key in he unlocked the door and walked inside. When he walked in the place was pitch black then he heard a male voice.

"Don't take another step or I'll blow your fucking head off." Danger spat.

"What do you want?" Halftime asked.

"It's not what I want. It's whom I want is the question. I want Justice and you're going to tell me where I can find him." Danger spat.

"I don't know nobody named Justice."

"How about you cut the lights on."

Halftime did as he was told, and flipped the switch. When the lights came on he dropped his grocery bags, and his face went pale as he seen his girl naked and tied up with his suitcase full of money and cocaine sitting neatly on the table.

"It's going to be okay baby." Halftime said trying his best to comfort Jazmine.

"That all depends on you." Danger spat. "Are you armed?"

"No." Halftime replied.

"Throw your keys on the floor, and take all of your clothes off."

"I'm not doing that. I don't know what type of shit you on, but I'm not with that freaky shit." Halftime said.

"You think this is a game, don't you boy?" Danger said pointing his gun at the girl head.

"Okay. Okay." Halftime said then began removing his clothes piece by piece until he was down to his boxers.

"Take your shoe strings out of your shoes, and throw them to me."

Halftime did as he was told. Danger got up, and walked toward Halftime grabbing him by the wrist. Halftime risking it spun around, and tried to take a swing at Danger knocking his gun out of his hand then he hit Danger with a quick right cross knocking him back. Danger shook his head looking up as Halftime tried to punch him again. Danger caught his fist in his hand, and spun Halftime's arm around his back at the same time kicking the back of his left knee cap, dropping Halftime to the ground. Grabbing his other .357 out of his holster Danger smacked him across the head knocking him unconscious. Making sure Halftime was knocked out he tied him up with a set of shoe strings Halftime had previously ripped out of his shoe. Walking to the bathroom Danger grabbed a curling iron that had to belong to Jazmine. He plugged it up inside the socket in the living room and let it get hot.

Splashing water on Halftime waking him up. Danger asked again.

"Where is Justice?"

"I don't know no Justice."

"Okay, that's how you wanta play."

Getting upset Danger walked over to the couch, and snatched a naked Jazmine by the hair then threw her on the floor next to Halftime.

"You see that hot iron over there warming up?" Danger uttered, grabbing Halftime by the head making him look at it.

"I'ma ask you one more time. If you lie to me again. I'ma stick that hot iron up your ass. Now tell me where is Justice?" Danger asked, as he went to retrieve the hot iron. When he returned he ripped the back of Halftimes boxers off. "I'm waiting." Danger spat while lowering the iron close to Halftimes butt cheeks.

"Okay, okay, please man don't do this to me." Halftime begged, feeling the heat around his ass as he shook in fear.

"I'm listening."

"He lives in a two story house on Bland Street." Halftime blurted out.

"What kind of car does he drive?"

"His girl drives a Benz, he drives a black Suburban, but he came into a bunch of money so it's no telling what he's driving now."

"Good, you see that wasn't hard, now I need you to give him a message for me." Danger spat sitting the hot iron down then walking over and picking his .357 off the ground that had hit the floor during their little scuffle.

"I'll tell him whatever you want, please just don't stick that damn iron in my ass." Halftime begged.

Danger stood behind Halftime and his Asian girlfriend. "Tell Justice this." Danger said as he raised his .357 and shot Halftime in the back of the head, his girlfriend Jazmine tried to scream but her sounds were muffled from her panties that were tied around her mouth.

"Now what should I do with you, pretty little birdie." Danger said as he empty his .357 dumping the remaining bullets into his hand. He stuck one bullet in the chamber and spent it around before closing it. "Just because I like you I'll give you one chance to live. A bullet never lies, if it clicks you live, if it doesn't well you already know you're dead honey." Raising his hand cannon he pulled the trigger. 'Click.' The sound made Jazmine pee on herself. Danger smiled to himself. "Congrads. Now you be still until I'm gone, and everything will be okay." Danger tucked his cannon back inside his holster, and walked out the door. Taking the steps two at a time knowing that he was pressed for time. When he got to the bottom of the steps he speed walked all the way back to his Nova. He got in and crunk the old Chevy up then slowly pulled out of the Castle Brooke Apartments, as he drove a line of police cruisers shot pass him.

After obtaining a no knock warrant Agent Slade had put the A.P.B out for Deion Harper. Currently they were headed to his last known address. Taking Harper into custody would bring him that much closer to bringing Justice and the Santiago crime syndicate down. Pulling into the parking lot of Castle Brooke Apartments, Agent Slade and multiple officers jumped out of their cars, and headed straight upstairs ramming the door down. Officers filled the room, and was surprised at what they seen, two people were laying on the floor naked and tied up. After the scene was clear Agent Slade walked in. "Untie this woman, and get her some clothes now." Agent Slade bellowed as he watched one of the officers untie her and the other one grabbed her a blanket. Agent Slade then pulled a paper from his back pocket which was a mugshot of Deion Harper AKA Halftime. He bent down and compared the mugshot to the dead body to confirm that it was in fact Deion Harper and it was. Agent Slade was furious. After having come so close to grabbing one of the suspects and a possible member of the Santiago syndicate. Looking over and seeing that the female was dressed he walked over to her.

"Ma'am, what is your name?" Agent Slade asked.

"Jazmine Williams."

"Are you okay, do you need medical attention?"

"No I'm okay."

"Is that your boyfriend on the floor?"

"Yes." Jazmine whispered.

"Can you tell me what happened?"

"Someone knocked on the door. I answered it, and was kicked in the chest. The guy pointed a gun at me, and demanded that I take all my clothes off. I did what he told me because I didn't wanta die." Jazmine paused and began to cry. "He came looking for Deion. When Deion came home he tied him up, and kept asking him about a guy name Justice."

"Justice you say?" Agent Slade asked.

"Yeah, he wanted to know where he could find him at."

"Did he tell him?"

"Yes, he told him, and he still killed him. I thought he was going to kill me. I still do he might come back."

"Jazmine you're safe now. Can you tell me what this guy looks like?"

"I don't know what he looks like he had a mask on." Jazmine lied not knowing why.

"Alright the officers here are going to take you down to the station so you can make a formal statement. Don't worry we'll get this guy and when we do he'll never see daylight again. I promise you that." Agent Slade said in all confidence, then he got up, and headed out to his truck.

Chapter 17

The Set Up

After taking care of her affairs in Charlotte, Maleekah headed to Chapel Hill, and began putting her plan into motion punching in the coordinates of Richard Murray and Associates in her GPS. She made the two and a half hour drive to Chapel Hill. After a lengthy drive Maleekah pulls into the parking lot of a plaza off Highway 54. She parked her Nissan Rogue then walked into the small law firm.

"Welcome to Richard Murray and Associates. I'm Lisa, how may I help you."

"I called earlier about a speeding ticket. I have a 1:30 appointment." Maleekah explained.

"If you don't mind me asking, what happened?"

"Well I moved here last week, and I was driving down 54 doing seventy. A state trooper was hidden off the side of the road. I couldn't slow down fast enough, and he pulled me over and the rest they say is history." Maleekah explained.

"Well I'm not trying to be a smart ass. If no one else said it, welcome to Chapel Hill home of the state troopers." Lisa replied playfully.

"Thank you." Maleekah answered as she busted out laughing.

"Hey Lisa I'm ready for my 1:30." Richard came out of his office and stated.

"Okay you can go to the back Mr. Murray is waiting for you." Lisa informed.

"Aite thank you." Maleekah replied walking to the back.

Twenty minutes later Maleekah came walking out of the back office and began heading to her car after she signed out, when Lisa stopped her.

"Look, since you're new in town would you like to have lunch? I know a spot that makes the best pork chop sandwiches in North Carolina." Lisa invited.

"Sure why not." Maleekah replied accepting her invitation.

"Okay hold up one second. Richard."

"Yeah."

"I'm on my way out, would you like anything?" Lisa asked punching the intercom.

"Umm, you going to Timeout?" Richard asked.

"Yeah." Lisa confirmed.

"Grab me a pork chop sandwich with coleslaw and onions on Texas toast."

"Okay I got you. I'll be back at 3:00pm."

"That's fine." Richard replied.

"Damn I know his breath is gonna be on fire." Maleekah joked as they jumped into Lisa's S550.

"Girl hush." Lisa busted out laughing.

"This a nice car."

"Thanks, my boyfriend makes pretty good money."

"Must be nice. Tell me what the hell is a time out?" Maleekah inquired.

"You'll find out in about five minutes." Lisa replied parking in front of the small diner. As usual Timeout was jumping with lunch time traffic everybody trying to get their grub on.

"Uh-huh girl, I know that ain't Michael Jordan holding up that sandwich in that picture." Maleekah asked amazed.

"I told you these sandwiches were the bomb. MJ went to school here at UNC. The cook made that sandwich for him on the spot, and all the tourist see that picture and gotta have one." Lisa said.

"Shit if all these celebs on the wall co-signed this place, then I'm already hooked." Maleekah chuckled as the two sat down with their plates, and ate their sandwiches.

"What is it to do around here?" Maleekah asked.

"We have a couple of bars around here and a few card houses out in the country. There's frat houses around on campus if you're into that type of stuff other than that everybody goes to Durham, Raleigh, or Greensboro to hit the clubs and party."

"Since I'm new here. I'm trying to get into a lil something. You're pretty cool why don't we hangout. I don't know nobody else around here."

"I don't really do much. I'm with my boyfriend most of the time."

"I know he has a few homeboys. I'm not trying to deal with no lames. Why don't you hook a sister up?"

"My man does have a few friends. I think I might have somebody for you, you'll like him he's down to earth, and likes to have fun."

"Well ya'll wanta try and get together this weekend?" Maleekah asked.

"Yeah we can, but let me holler at my man first and see what he has planned. I'll get back with you on that." Lisa answered.

"Okay that'll be fine. Just let me know."

"I'll do that, are you ready?" Lisa asked. After seeing the cook hold Richards bag up.

"Yeah, I'm full as hell." Maleekah admitted. Then both girls got up, and headed to the register, and paid for their meals. Lisa grabbed Richard's bag and they both headed out and jumped in Lisa's S550. When they got back to the place the two exchanged information said their goodbyes as Maleekah got in her Nissan Rogue and left.

'Ring' 'Ring' 'Ring'.
"Yo." Justice answered.
"Sorry to bother you bro, but Halftime was killed sometime this morning." Red Bull informed.
"What, are you sure?"
"Yeah, I got a call from Jaz, she's scared as hell too bruh."
"What happened?"
"She said some big guy kicked her in the chest when she opened the door. He made her get naked and robbed her and waited for Halftime to come home. Jaz said the guy kept asking Halftime about you."
"What did Halftime tell him?"
"She didn't say bruh, she said to tell you to be careful."
"Okay, give her fifty thousand. Tell her to leave town. I don't want her involved in no police investigations, tell her to go on vacation. I'll call her personally in a couple of days."
"What you wanna do about the bro?" Red Bull asked.
"Put the soldiers on the streets find out who did this. My guy is telling me it's Money-B's people, but we need to be sure."
"Are you good over there?"
"Yeah, I'm bout to move to Burlington in Kanden's old place."
"I think that's smart. You don't need to be in Chapel Hill no more."
"That's a big fact. I just gotta try to get Lisa to quit her job. We don't need the money she just loves to work."
"I suggest you make a job for her. Let her run the books or something, so you can keep a eye on her."
"Yeah she's been asking, how are you coming along with

Amir's Mexican friends?"

"Everything good since you plugged him in with ya boy in Atlanta, shits been running more smooth."

"So you saying it wasn't running smooth when I was driving?"

"Nah big bro I ain't saying that. It's just we don't have to stress as much. We need you out here. Not on the highway taking chances, that's what you got us for."

"That's peace bruh. Look I gotta put something together. I know Halftime was your man. Make sure his funeral is paid for and his mother is good. On my dime homie."

"Aite I'ma do that."

"Keep me informed." Justice said before hanging up.

Later that evening when Lisa got home from work she was surprised that Justice was at home and not out on business. He sat in front of the T.V. watching the 6 o'clock news drinking a Miller Highlife.

"Hey baby." Lisa said, as she sat her pocketbook down on the table and walked over and sat on the couch next to her man.

"What's up luv, how was your day?" Justice asked.

"It was okay. I met a girl named Maleekah today. She just moved into town she came by the office. We talked a lil bit, and went out for lunch after she met with Richard."

"Sounds like you had a eventful day."

"Yeah, she wanted to hook up with one of your friends."

"What, baby you know I don't be doing stuff like that."

"I know, but you know I don't have any friends, and I want to get out of the house and have a lil fun."

"I have a lot of things going on right now."

"That's why we need to get out of the house and do something to take your mind off business." Lisa stated.

"What do you have in mind then?"

"I want you to hook Maleekah up with Amir. Maybe we can

go out to eat or go to the movies or something."

"Baby you don't even know this girl all that well."

"I know but she cool, plus I wanta go out and have some fun."

"I don't know about this."

"Baby please I wanta go out this weekend. Just one time that's all I'm asking." Lisa begged as she began to rub Justice crotch massaging the bulge in his pants. Feeling his penis harden she unbutton his pants and pulled his dick out. Lowering her head down she kissed the tip of his penis then slowly stuck the head in her mouth bobbing her head up and down and side to side all while staring Justice in the eyes. When he closed them she stopped slowly sliding his dick out of her mouth she knew she had him. "You going to take me out this weekend?" Lisa whispered.

"Yes baby don't stop I got you." Justice replied.

"Thank you." Lisa said lowering her head back down taking his penis back in her mouth.

Danger pulled up on Bland Street he searched the road endlessly until he found what he was looking for. When he did he parked a couple of houses down and waited. Seeing a sexy white girl with an ass to rival Buffy getting out of a Mercedes Benz and walking into a two story home he knew then that he was at the right place. So he waited longer it seemed like hours before he saw anybody come out of the house, then his target stepped out. He could tell by the pictures that it was Justice, he had stepped out to walk his pit. This would be like taking candy from a baby Danger thought as he checked his hand cannons. He continued to look on and was about to make a move until he saw an old Chevy 62 Impala drop top pull up, then he watched as Justice picked his pit bull up and sat him in the back seat, then he himself walked over to the passenger seat and got inside the car. Danger continued to watch as the old Impala pulled off slowly it's driver hitting the switches causing the old Chevy to bounce up and down. Being that this was the right place, Danger laid his seat back to get comfortable as he waited for Justice to return.

After his sex marathon with Lisa Justice had called Harlem World and Amir letting them both know what Red Bull had told him. Amir had sent Harlem World to pick Justice up. Playing it off not wanting to scare Lisa he told her he was going to walk his dog and clear his head that he'll be back in a couple of hours. After walking out of the house with his pit in tow he looked around and noticed an old Nova parked down the street that he had never seen before. Not really paying it any mind figuring it was one of his neighbors many street drag cars he walked up the street and met with Harlem, after getting inside the old Impala they headed to the Dirt Road to meet Amir.

When they pulled up Amir had the fire burning inside an old metal barrel, and was sitting on the hood of his Cutlass, as he serves his feins, and smoked a blunt. Harlem and Justice got out then Justice picked up his dog out of the back seat and sat him on the ground and unclipped his leash letting him roam free. They both walked up to Amir and dapped him up.

"Yo they got Halftime bruh." Justice said.

"That shit crazy as hell, we gotta make a move." Amir replied.

"I'm ready to clean these nikkas up." Harlem World stated ready for action.

"I know bro but we gotta find these guys first." Justice said.

"They're going to pop up sooner or later. We just gotta wait them out. Our soldiers will bring some info back." Amir replied.

"I understand that, but by the time they do, one of us could be taken out because we can't see them coming. I wanta stare death in the eye, and die on my feet feel me." Harlem World spat.

"I feel you bruh, it won't come to that tho." Justice replied.

"How you figure?" Harlem asked.

"I'ma send the soldiers to clean Clara Cox out turn that shit into a desert." Amir stated with venom in his voice.

"That's not smart the feds will be on us in no time then." Justice said. "What we're going to do is hold back. When something solid reaches us we'll move on it then. How's everything been going with my boys in the A?" Justice asked.

"Business is booming, Red Bull's dealing with the Mexicans now, Torres likes him. I got your cut in the safe." Amir answered.

"Nah bro you good, Kanden left me super straight. When all this bullshit blows over I'ma have something nice for you, Harlem and Bull."

"Yeah, that peace." Amir replied as he passed Justice the blunt. "Be careful that's the gas right there."

Back on Bland Street Lisa called Maleekah, after she had gotten out of the shower.

Ring ring.

"Hey girl." Maleekah answered picking up on the second ring.

"What's going on, you busy?"

"Nah, I ain't doing nothing. Just sitting here reading the new Durell Eubanks book I Am Tony Blanco."

"Is it good?" Lisa asked.

"Yeah it's urban fiction, what's going on with you?"

"It's a date for Friday." Lisa said sounding excited.

"Okay, the dude better not be a mud duck. I'll walk out of that joint." Maleekah scolded.

"Girl I promise you'll like him. Wear something cute, you wanta go shopping tomorrow?" Lisa asked.

"Now what kinda friend would I be to turn down that invitation?"

"That's what's up I'll pick you up around ten. We'll make a day out of it."

"Sounds good to me."

"Aite then I'll let you get back to your book."

"That's what's up me and Tom got plans for tonight." Maleekah replied.

"Tom." Lisa asked puzzled.

"Yeah girl my dildo." Maleekah laughed.

"Girl you silly as hell, see you tomorrow." Lisa couldn't contain her laughter.

"Cough, cough, cough, damn this shit is some gas." Justice said passing the blunt to Harlem World who pulled it and held the smoke like it was nothing."

"I'ma professional, I should get paid for this shit." Harlem World said then continued hitting the blunt.

"Yo Amir I need you Friday." Justice stated.

"I got you what's up?" Amir asked.

"Lisa met some girl at her office that just moved here, she wants to go out on a double date."

"You sure that's smart right now?" Amir asked.

"No, but my girl has a way of getting what she wants. I gave her my word." Justice answered.

"I got cha, what's the girl's name?"

"Maleekah."

"She better not be ugly man."

"Trust I told Lisa the same thing."

"Just let me know then." Amir stated.

"I'll do that. Look tho, I gotta get back to the house." Justice said and then called for his dog who came running as soon as he heard his master's voice. Justice clamped the leash on his collar then picked him up and sat him in the backseat of Harlem's Impala. Harlem World and Justice dapped Amir up then headed out.

Danger sat inside his Nova as he watched the old Impala pull back up and drop Justice off. Looking at his wrist he checked his watched it was nine thirty. Still too early to make his move he thought to himself, as he caressed his beloved cannons. Deciding to wait for the right time he sat back in his seat. Rechecking his watch a couple of hours later it was now one in the morning. Danger rolled his window down and looked at the house seeing that all the lights were off inside. He opened the door to his old Chevy and got out. Walking slowly towards the three bedroom house Danger removed one of his three fifty sevens and ducked low as he lightly jogged across the front yard making it to the side of the house. Danger began peeping through the windows. When he got to the last window he noticed that it was cracked, so he peeped inside. Justice was not asleep, he sat in a recliner chair with an M-16 laid across his lap, as if he was waiting for someone to come for him. As Danger continued to look thru the window at Justice he could tell that the man he hunted was not afraid. Deciding that the element of surprise was gone Danger slowly disappeared into the darkness as he headed back to his car. Deciding to strike another time.

CHAPTER 18

LIFE OF THE PARTY

The next morning Lisa got up early and got dressed leaving Justice snoring in the bed tired from having been up all night. When he had gotten back home she noticed that he had been acting kinda weird. She had even checked on him around two o'clock in the morning and found him wide awake with this huge gun laying across his lap smoking a blunt in the dark. He didn't see her at least he didn't act like he did. She took a mental note to talk to him later. Maybe the double date tonight would help him relieve some unwanted stress. Checking her purse Lisa made sure she had her keys and her credit cards as she headed out the door. Lisa got into her S550 Benz and pulled off listening to some old Alicia Keys. After a twenty minute drive she turned into Lake Hill Apartments. Excited that she had made a new friend and knew that once Amir saw Maleekah he'd be stuck. Lisa parked and got out of her car grabbing her purse, she headed to Maleekah's apartment. Knocking on the door Maleekah opened up. The placed smelled like breakfast.

"Hey come in." Maleekah invited.

"Dang girl you got it smelling like IHOP up in here." Lisa said surprised.

"Shit IHOP can't fuck with me." Maleekah stated cockily. "You hungry? Mi casa su casa go ahead and fix you a plate."

"Shoot you don't have to tell me twice." Lisa answered grabbing herself a plate and filling it until the food was falling off the sides.

"Go ahead and eat I'll be ready in fifteen minutes." Maleekah instructed.

"Mmm hmm." Lisa mumbled her mouth full of food.

"Fifteen minutes later Maleekah came out wearing a beige and black Saint Lauren pantsuit with a pair of black heels and a matching pocketbook.

"Look at you number one stunna." Lisa said joking.

"I like to do my thing a lil." Maleekah replied walking over to the kitchen and putting the dishes in the dishwasher.

Then they both headed out the door. The pair jumped in Lisa's whip, and pulled off heading to the mall. The conversation between them flowed easily talking the whole way and only stopping when Lisa pulled into the Hanes Mall parking lot. Getting out going inside they went store to store looking for something to wear tonight. When it was all said and done they ended up running thru twelve bands. Lisa bought a red and gold Vera Wang strapless dress with a pair of six-inch gold stilettos. While Maleekah picked out a dark brown spaghetti strapped Versace gown as well as a pair of dark brown heels. After the two finished shopping they ended up at the hair salon and spa.

Exhausted the two headed back. Lisa dropped Maleekah to get a few zzz's and get ready for tonight.

"Girl I haven't had that much fun in a minute." Maleekah gracefully said. "Me either. I'll see you tonight. I'll come back thru, and pick you up. We'll meet them there."

"Aite see you later." Maleekah said while giving Lisa a hug before she left. Later that night Lisa went and picked up Maleekah and headed to their destination. Club Onyx was the spot on Friday nights, everybody who was somebody was there. If you was a baller then you were definitely in the building. When Lisa and Maleekah walked inside all eyes were on them as they both walked through the crowd. Sitting down at their reserved table they ordered their drinks, as they sat, and waited for their dates to arrive. When Justice and Amir strolled in looking like the hoodstars they were giving hugs and daps to a few of the people they knew as they bopped to the table. Seeing her man coming Lisa stood up and gave Justice a hug and a kiss then introduced Justice and Amir to Maleekah. After the introductions were made Lisa was glad to see that Maleekah and Amir seemed to have instant chemistry. When the Deejay started playing a new song by NBA Youngboy Maleekah got up from the table and grabbed Amir by the arm.

"Come on this my joint right here." Maleekah said excitedly leading Amir to the dance floor.

"Come on baby. We might as well hit the dance floor too." Lisa said.

"Think you can keep up?" Justice shot back smoothly.

"Boy please, you know I ain't the average white girl." Lisa replied cockily grabbing Justice by the arm pulling him to the dance floor beside Maleekah and Amir. As both couple danced Maleekah began to take over the dance floor twirling, twisting, bending, and shaking her ass. A circle formed around her the crowd cheering her on.

"Damn." Justice slipped out seeing Maleekah's ass shake. "The girl can bust a move." He recovered quickly after seeing Lisa's eyes shoot darts at him.

"I know right." Lisa said as the song ended and people started clapping as Maleekah and Amir walked back to the table where Lisa and Justice awaited them.

"Girl, where did you learn to get down like that?" Lisa asked as Maleekah and Amir sat down.

"I went to A&T you know Aggie Pride. I majored in communications and minored in performing arts." Maleekah replied.

"That's what's up." Amir stated.

"Damn right." Justice said backing Amir up with his compliment.

"What made you want to move to Chapel Hill?" Amir asked full of curiosity.

"I was in a relationship for three years, one day I woke up and felt like it wasn't going anywhere. I tried to break it off. My ex got angry and punched me in the face breaking my jaw in three places. After that I had to eat out of a straw for months until my jaw healed. I end up pressing charges. I was just so tired of the abuse and I didn't know any other way to get out. I fully recovered. I saved my money and moved away." Maleekah answered giving her fake background story.

"That's fucked up." Amir stated shaking his head in disgust.

"Damn girl much respect for getting yourself outta that situation." Justice said.

"You know we gotcha back." Lisa replied.

"Don't worry about it, it's over and done with now. I'm starting a new chapter in my life." Maleekah said waving her hand dismissively.

"Sho you right." Lisa replied giving Maleekah a high five.

"Okay enough of revealing my baggage. What does everyone wants to drink? This round on me." Maleekah said as she stood up.

"Bud light." Justice requested.

"Henny and Coke." Amir added.

"Another Long Island Ice Tea for me." Lisa ordered.

"Okay I'll be right back." Maleekah said as she left to get the groups drinks. Fifteen minutes Maleekah returned with everyone's drinks on a tray.

"Guess what guys?" Maleekah asked full of excitement, as she sat the tray on the table.

"What's up girl?" Lisa asked wondering what her new friend was so excited about.

"I just got a job." Maleekah shot back.

"Get the fuck outta here." Justice said in disbelief.

"Damn you move fast." Amir quizzed.

"How'd you do that?" Lisa asked.

"I struck up a convo with the manager about drinks while I was waiting on ours. I told him I was a walking bartending bible." Maleekah explained.

"If that's what you like then congratulations on your new beginning." Justice stated raising his glass for a toast.

"Here, here." Amir and Lisa raised their glasses.

"Dang I almost forgot I start Tuesday." Maleekah added finishing the good news off. Everyone was happy for what looked like the newest member of the bunch. They all sat and talked for a while until the last call for alcohol was made. Everyone made plans to go out to the movies the weekend after next to see the new Star Wars movie. When the lights came on and let the club out everyone said their goodbyes. Justice rode back with Lisa since Amir had driven his BMW Maleekah chose to ride with him so she could work her magic alone.

Justice had fallen asleep during the drive home. When they pulled into the driveway Lisa woke him up and they both went inside. After getting undressed and comfortable they both laid on their king size bed.

"You know your girl seems cool but…" Justice let the statement hang in the air.

"Go ahead. But what." Lisa inquired.

"She just pops up outta nowhere, I mean what do you really know about her?" Justice asked the obvious question.

"Why do you gotta be so critical and suspicious of everyone?" Lisa asked a question of her own.

"In the line of business we're in it pays to be suspicious." Justice reasoned.

"I know but dang." Lisa said frustrated.

"I'm just saying we don't know anything about shorty. See if you can get your boss to do a background check on her."

"Okay I will. Personally I don't think everyone is out to hurt you or get you baby."

"Amir's friend Deion was murdered the other day, I know you seen it on the news."

"Yeah I seen it. I thought it was just a random robbery."

"No they were looking for me."

"What, what's going on Justice? You were up all night last night. I got up to go to the bathroom. I saw you sitting in your recliner with your gun laying across your lap."

"I couldn't sleep. Becoming head of the family has been stressful. I'm moving us to Burlington tomorrow to my brother's mansion."

"This is our home. I paid for this with everything I had."

"I understand that but I can't protect you here and it's too dangerous for you to be here alone. I'm moving you to a better place more security. I want you to quit your job we're leaving Chapel Hill."

"What if I don't wanta leave?"

"Lisa I love you and you know that." Justice said as he caressed Lisa face he paused. "With the money we have now we can go anywhere in the world. I just need you safe while I finish this war. When it's finished we'll leave Burlington or even North Carolina if you want. I'll buy a yacht and we can live on the water if that's what will make you happy. I just want you safe. I need to be certain." Justice explained.

"I understand baby. I just want say so in the matter." Lisa stated.

"I respect that I really do, but I just can't leave it up to chance." Justice paused. "I couldn't live with myself if something happened to you because of what I've done or my families past beefs."

"I know." Lisa agreed. "But God has protected us this long why would he stop now?"

"You know I'm not a religious person, so don't start preaching. I made a promise and I intend on keeping it end of discussion. Now lay down so we can get us some rest we have a big day tomorrow."

Chapter 19

Devils Die Too

Saturday morning Justice called Vinny, Kanden's old bodyguard.

'Ring'.

"Yeah." Vinny picked up on the first ring.

"I want you to get a couple guys over. I want everything moved out and into Kanden's old place pronto." Justice demanded.

"I'm on it sir, I'll have everything at the mansion ready for your arrival is there anything else that you need?" Vinny asked.

"No, that'll be all for now, thanks." Justice said before hanging up.

Walking into the kitchen Justice leaned over and hugged Lisa as she sat on a stool drinking a cup of coffee.

"It'll be okay baby you'll like the new place."

"I don't know, this is home right here. We have so many memories here in this house this is where our son passed."

"I know, we'll make new memories. It's time for us to have a clean slate you deserve that after all we been through."

"Maybe you're right Justice you know me better than anyone. All I ask of you is that we don't sell the place or rent it out. I want to leave it like it is. All I wanta take is our clothes."

"Baby I just got off the phone with Vinny he's sending some people over to pack our things and take them to the new place. I promise you we won't sell or rent this place out. I'll tell you what: I'll even pay somebody to come by every week to mow the yard and keep the place up and you can come by here whenever you like."

"That will be nice." Lisa said as she got up and rubbed her stomach.

"What's wrong babe?"

"Nothing just feeling a lil sick, I'ma go pack."

"Aite, I have to go make a few runs. Vinny will be over in a few, okay?"

"Be careful." Lisa said disappearing into the back.

Looking out the window Lisa watched as Justice left, again missing the chance to tell him that she was pregnant. Closing the curtains, she walked over to the dresser, and picked up her phone needing someone to talk to she dialed Maleekah.

"Hey girl." Maleekah picked up on the fourth ring.

"Hey! I just called to see how you were doing." Lisa said.

"I'm good me and Amir hit it off good last night, so I'm kinda tired."

"He stayed the night?"

"Yeah, he just left. I know what you're thinking and no we didn't do anything. We just sat up and talked all night."

"Me and Justice did the same thing, he's talking about moving."

"Moving."

"Yeah."

"Moving where?" Maleekah asked trying to get more info out of her.

"To his late brother's place in Burlington."

"I know you're not trying to do that."

"No I'm really not. He just gets me so mad sometimes." Lisa admitted with frustration in her voice.

"I guess he just wants the best for you."

"Have you been taping our conversations? You sound just like him." Lisa asked playfully.

"You think I work for the feds?" Maleekah shot back.

"Girl I'm just playing, it's just sometimes he can be so controlling. I can't stand it." Lisa replied not letting it go.

"You know you can always come over here and chill with me whenever you like."

"Thanks Maleekah, you know, I'm glad I met you. I don't have too many friends."

"I'm glad I met you too whenever you come over we can make it a girl's night." Maleekah reasoned.

"You trying to get me in trouble, Justice would never let me stay out all night. It sounds like it would be fun tho."

"It will, you could show me the city you know I'm new here."

"Yeah that's true let me think on it, and I'll let you know what I'm going to do."

"Okay you do that."

"I'll talk to you later." Lisa said before hanging up.

After Maleekah hung the phone up with Lisa she immediately called Rondo.

'Ring' 'Ring' 'Ring'.

"What up lil mama." Rondo answered after the third ring.

"I've got some news." Maleekah answered.

"What's the business is talk to me?" Rondo said.

"Lisa's man ya boy Justice, he's moving them to Burlington to his late brother's house. Lisa's pretty pissed about it. I'm trying to talk her into coming over here for girl's night." Maleekah explained.

"His brother's house you say?"

"Yeah I don't have the address yet, but give me a few more days and I'll get it."

"I know the address, look you go ahead and head back to Charlotte. I'll wire your money to you."

"You sure baby? I can get more info if needed. His boy Amir spent the night over here last night. I couldn't get much outta him tho, he'll be a lil harder to work."

"I'm sure you're good, you've already gotten me everything I need."

"Aite, you coming to see me when I get back right?"

"Of course Maleekah you know that, but I'ma wire you that bread first, so I won't have to hear your mouth."

"Okay baby I'll see you soon." Maleekah chuckled before hanging up.

Getting off the phone with Maleekah, Rondo flipped through his call log until he landed on Danger's number then he hit send.

'Ring' 'Ring' 'Ring' 'Ring'.

"Yo." Danger answered on the third ring.

"How is everything coming along with the mark?" Rondo asked.

"Everything is going according to plan. I'm sitting in front of his house now. Justice just left his girl is alone in the house."

"I just got off the phone with one of my contacts. He supposed to be moving into his brother's mansion in Burlington. If he does that you won't be able to get to him."

"No worries I'm bout to wrap this shit up. Good look on the info tho." Danger said before hanging up. Rondo looked at his phone after hearing the dial tone. I'ma kill that mutha fucka when this is all over. Rondo thought to himself. Rolling over in his bed wrapping his arms around the two naked Mexican girls waking them up for another round.

Danger sat in his Nova and watched the house for another two hours before deciding to make his move. No one had been in and out of the house since Justice had left. Danger checked his watch it was almost three o'clock. Pulling one of his hand cannons out of the holster he popped the three-fifty-sevens chamber out and spent it around then slapped it shut. Figuring he'll kidnap the girl, then wait for Justice to come home. He exited his Nova with his three fifty seven in his hand. Slowly he walked over to Justices house, taking the easy approach being that it was broad daylight. He walked straight up to the front door, before knocking he checked the door knob to his surprise it was unlocked, slowly he turned the knob and pushed the door open. Pulling his mask over his face he walked inside.

Lisa was inside her walk-in closet packing when she heard the sound of the front door opening.
"Justice." Lisa hollered. "Is that you baby?"
No one answered.
"Vinny you there, is that you?" Lisa hollered. Still no one answered. Remembering what Justice had told her Lisa walked out of her closet and into her bedroom walking over to her bed she reached under the pillow, and grabbed her .380 slowly she cocked it letting a bullet slide into the chamber. Placing two hands on the butt of the pistol she slowly walked out of the bedroom, and began walking down the hall. Looking at the mirror Lisa saw the image of a huge man with a black ski-mask over his face. Ducking down she got as close to him as she could without being seen. When she had a clear view, she raised her gun at the intruder and pulled the trigger.

Walking through the house Danger heard Lisa call out for Justice, then she called out for a guy named Vinny. He realized that she had been expecting company. Taking two more steps he heard a loud gunshot then felt the pressure knocking him to the floor touching his right shoulder, his left hand was smeared with blood as he realized he had been hit.

"Get the fuck outta my house." Danger heard the girl yell. Raising his three fifty seven he returned fire sending two rounds into her direction leaving two big holes in the wall. Danger got to his feet and ducked low. Slowly he tried to stand to see if he could get a clear view of where the girl was shooting from.

'Bloc', 'Bloc'. Danger ducked as bullets flew over his head. "Shit, shit." He said to himself frustrated that he had been discovered knowing by the sound of the gun he knew she was shooting a small caliber pistol. Danger snatched up a wooden chair and slung it into the hall shooting two more rounds at the same time running to the hallway. He caught sight of the girl as she ran back into the bedroom firing two more rounds at him barely missing his face. Danger leaned on the wall as he gained ground.

"Come out now and I won't hurt you."

"Fuck you mutha fucka, get outta my house."

"I don't want to kill you, but I will if you make me. I'm not here for you."

"I know what you're here for."

'Bloc' 'Bloc' 'Bloc'. Three more round flew in Dangers direction. This girl is crazy Danger thought to himself. Then he heard a group of voices in the living room.

Vinny and four other soldiers pulled up at the house. When they got out of their SUV's instantly they heard the gunshots, they all went straight into actions pulling their Glocks as they rushed into the house.

"Lisa." Vinny yelled from the living room.

"Yeah." Lisa hollered back happy to hear Vinny's voice.

"Where are you? Are you hurt?" Vinny hollered.

"I'm in the bedroom. I'm pinned down. I'm okay. The bastard's in the hallway." Lisa yelled.

"Okay stay put we're coming for you." Vinny hollered. "Aite let's move, you over here you over there, you two cover me." Vinny gave directions as he moved in. 'Bloc' 'Bloc' 'Bloc'. Vinny fired three rounds from his forty cal trying to get the intruder to reveal his position, and just as Vinny thought the intruder returned fire.

'Boom' 'Boom'. Danger shot back.

"He's in the hallway, you move." Vinny said signaling for one of his soldiers to hit the hallway. The soldier complied, and Vinny fell in right behind him. The masked man shot two revolvers at the same time towards Vinny. The soldier was hit in the neck, but Vinny caught him and held him up like a shield as he fired back hitting the masked man in the knee cap dropping him to the ground. Seeing this Lisa slid out of the bedroom. She pointed her gun at the back of the masked man's head and pulled the trigger. 'Bloc'. The single shot from her .380 rang out as Dangers lifeless body fell to the floor. Making sure the intruder was dead Vinny fired another round in the man's chest before walking over to Lisa and making sure she was okay.

"Give me your phone." Lisa asked.

Vinny handed it over without question.

Lisa punched in Justices number and pressed the send button. 'Ring' 'Ring'.

"Vinny what's up?"

"This isn't Vinny it's Lisa come home now. I need you." Lisa said.

"What's wrong baby, talk to me." Justice replied.

"Not over the phone just come home now." Lisa said, and then hung up, and handed Vinny back his phone. He grabbed it then walked over to the dead body and pulled the dead man's mask up so he could see who he was. When he did he immediately recognized the man. "Danger." Vinny whispered knowing that his old friend was sent by none other than Rondo.

"Do you know him?" Lisa asked.

"Yeah we did two tours in Iraq together. He saved my team once, he shot a radical terrorist before he could fire a RPG at our Humvee."

"Why was he here at my house?"

"Rondo sent him to kill Justice."

"Who is Rondo?"

"That's his employer. Me and this guy were friends. We just work for two different sides."

30 minutes later Justice came storming through the door.

"Yo what the fuck, Lisa where are you?" Justice hollered after seeing the two bodies on the floor.

"She's out back sitting on the porch."

"What the fuck happened?" Justices asked Vinny wanting to know before he went out to see his girl.

"When we pulled up we heard gunshots and came rushing in. The intruder had Lisa pinned down. We moved in he took one of us down. I shot him then Lisa killed him." Vinny explained.

"Lisa killed that man?"

"Yes sir."

"Okay get rid of the bodies."

"You don't want me to call the police?"

"Fuck no Vinny, I don't want the police snooping around."

"Okay I'll take care of it." Vinny said. "Ya'll heard the boss let's get to work. You grab that carpet over there let's get these bodies outta here, and this place cleaned up." Vinny ordered.

The remaining three soldiers around him seeing that Vinny had everything in order Justice walked out on the porch to check on Lisa. Walking through the slider door Lisa was sitting on the steps with her .380 on the ground beside her.

"Are you okay baby?" Justice asked.

"I'm fine but the guy inside laying in our hallway isn't."

"Don't worry about him, that is being taken care of."

"Vinny said that man came here to kill you, that he was sent by some guy name Rondo. I wanta know what's going on Justice. I just took a man's life." Lisa said as she began to cry.

Justice walked over and sat down beside her putting his arm around her neck, and pulling her close.

"I want to know everything Justice. I mean it you can trust me."

"I do trust you." Justice replied. "Listen baby I'll tell you everything, but first I wanta get you outta here. Let's go to Burlington when we get to the mansion. I'll tell you everything I promise."

"You promise."

"Yes baby." Justice said as he help Lisa to her feet and picking her gun up off the ground they both walked inside, Justice handed Lisa's gun to Vinny.

"Get rid of this too."

"Okay."

"Another thing who the fuck is Rondo?"

"He's Money-B's right hand." Vinny answered.

"I want to know everything about him. When this is cleaned up come see me." Justice replied as he headed to the door with Lisa, they both got in the car headed to Burlington.

Chapter 20

King of Spades

At Kanden's mansion deep down on Maple Ave past all the hotels the place looked like a ranch there were horses and tractors. Then far off into the field broken off into it's own section there were cows. Pulling down farther until he was in front of the house they both got out and were met by two female housekeepers.

"How are you doing sir my name is Asia, and this is my sister Alicia. We are the housekeepers here."

"Nice to meet you." Lisa greeted.

Justice looked up, and saw six other guys dressed in suits.

"What are they?" Justice asked.

"They're the security of course." Asia answered.

"They must work with Vinny. How bout we go inside, and you can show us around."

"Follow me." Alicia said leading the way inside.

When they walked inside the place was huge probably three times the size of their three bedroom home. The sisters lead the way showing them every room. The place was nice six bedrooms, two bathrooms, a huge living room, a weight room and spa equipped with all the newest weights, and a mini theater. The sisters led them outside to the back of the house there was land for days there was also a garage.

"We cannot go inside there, but you can since this place is yours now, here are the keys." Asia said handing Justice the key ring.

"What's inside?" Lisa asked.

"Mr. Santiago's old car collection." Alicia answered.

Justice looked at Lisa, then he stuck the key inside the lock, and opened the door and walked inside. He looked to the left and saw a switch, so he flipped it, the lights instantly came on. There was a new Benz, a Corvette, a 745 BMW, a Jaguar, an old Dodge Viper, a 2015 Suzuki Hayabusa, a chromed out Harley Davidson, and two Caddies, an old sixties model and a 2017. After briefly looking around Justice cut the lights back off, and he and Lisa walked back outside and back inside the house letting the two sisters continue doing their daily duties.

Inside Justice sat Lisa down, he told her everything he knew of his family's secrets and everything that he had done to gain the power that he now had. After hearing everything Lisa was not surprised. She knew her man like the back of her hand. She knew he would do anything for that mighty dollar. What was understood needed not to be explained between them, they weren't married but they were one within itself. A few hours later Vinny came walking through the door.

"Where is Mr. Santiago?" Vinny asked the housekeeper.

"He's downstairs in the game room playing pool." Asia answered and then watched as Vinny headed that direction. Vinny walked into the game room with his head held high.

"Everything has been taken care of sir, is the lady okay?" Vinny asked.

"She's fine, upstairs sleeping. Have a seat I need to speak with you."

Vinny sat down Justice then sat the pool stick on the table and sat down across from him.

"I know, I am new at this." Justice said, as he waved his hand around. "I'm not used to all this fancy stuff. I was raised in the streets. I worked and killed for everything I've ever owned. Even the position I now hold as head of the Santiago family. I killed for this. Nothing was ever given to me. Now this is where you listen to me very carefully, understand?"

Vinny nodded his head.

"I do not like secrets, do you understand that Vinny?"

"Yeah I understand."

"Okay, now that you do. I want you to tell me everything about my enemy."

"I don't know much about Rondo except that he was Money-B's general. Now that Money-B been disposed of. I know that Rondo has taken over, I know he sent Danger to kill you."

"How do you know Danger?"

"We did two tours in Iraq together. We fought together he saved my life. We became friends once we returned to the states, as time went by we lost contact with each other. Then the family war broke out. I joined your brother and Danger joined Money-B. The lines were drawn. We never spoke after that, and I haven't seen him until today."

"I see, do you know where I can find Rondo?"

"He's probably staying in Money-B's mansion in Charlotte."

"Do you know where that is?"

"No, but someone in Clara Cox will know."

"Then we'll grab someone from there and make them tell us. I'ma call Amir, and Harlem World. I want you to meet them somewhere in Burlington, and bring them here." Justice replied picking his phone up off the table and dialing Amir's number.

'Ring' 'Ring'.

"Justice, what up?" Amir answered.

"Not too much, somebody tried to hit Lisa today."

"Is she okay?"

"Yeah, she's a soldier. Look I'm no longer in Chapel Hill, I'm in Burlington at my brother's old place."

"Bout time you made that move."

"I'm glad I did it before it was too late, right now I need you and Harlem World to meet Vinny so he can bring you both back to the mansion. We have much to discuss."

"If you don't mind me asking, who is Vinny?"

"He was Kanden's bodyguard. He now works closely with me."

"Alright enough said, right now I'm getting everything ready for Red Bull so he can meet Torres with the hammers. I'ma wrap this up then I'm on the way, I'll call when we get to Burlington."

"I'll be waiting." Justice replied and then hung up.

"Amir will call when he's in Burlington you can go out and meet them then." Justice said to Vinny as he stood up and walked back over to the pool table and finished his game.

Midafternoon Rondo sat at Money-B's desk as he counted the six thousand that BG had brought him that he received from LA before he was killed. As they both sat and talked, Rondo explained to BG what he expected out of him as his general. Just as he began to speak about Justice and his plan to have him murdered his phone began to ring. Rondo picked it up. The voice on the other end sent chills through his body. "Rondo is Justice dead?" King Charles asked.

"Mr. Charles, huh how are you?"

"I'm well, why haven't you answered my question yet? You should know I don't like repeating myself."

"He is not dead yet sir, but he will be soon. I have my best man onto him. I'm going to get him before he moves into Kanden's mansion."

"You've had enough time. I'm sending Rahman to pick you up and bring you to Atlanta we need to have a face to face mind you, you know the consequences for your family if you try to duck this meeting."

"Sir I assure you that everything will be-"

"Click."

Rondo heard the dial tone before he could finish his sentence.

After hanging up on Rondo, King Charles summoned his general Ra'mon waving him over as he sat in his old rocking chair smoking a cigar.

"Ra'mon, I want you to have your brother go and pick Rondo up and bring him here."

"Sir he has only been back a few days."

"I know I'm sure he won't mind tho." King Charles replied staring him directly in the eyes.

"Of course sir." Ra'mon replied knowing better than to push further.

"Another thing, bring me my tablet I need to facetime Vincente Flaco. Come to find out Phatom has been selling guns to Justice and his partner Amir, they are selling them to the Mexican gangs in Durham." King Charles said and then laughed as Ra'mon left to get his tablet.

"Who was that boss?" BG asked Rondo.

"Someone that you never want to meet." Rondo answered while picking his phone up. He dialed Dangers number. 'Ring' 'Ring' 'Ring' 'Ring'. "Shit." Rondo said to himself as Danger's voicemail came on. Rondo hung up then tried calling again still no one answered. "What the fuck is this mutha fucka doing?" Rondo said out loud slamming his fist on the table in frustration

CARTEL CITY

knowing his life was on the line.

"Is everything okay?" BG asked.

"Yeah everything's good, I want you and some of your guys to head down to Burlington." Rondo said while writing down the address to Kanden's mansion then handed it to BG.

"I want ya'll to case the place out call me and tell me what you see when you get there."

"Who am I looking for?"

"A guy name Justice, he's Mexican and black, short haircut, and stocky. You'll know him when you see him.

"What do you want us to do if we see him?"

"You won't be able to get to the mansion because of the security. Wait til he leaves then take him out make sure it's messy."

"Okay, I'ma get that done for you but my boys will expect payment."

"That's not a problem just get it done."

BG nodded then got up and walked out of Rondo's office.

A few hours later Amir and Harlem World were pulling into the Citco gas parking lot. Amir pulled out his phone and called Justice.

'Ring' 'Ring'.

"Yo." Justice answered.

"We're in Burlington."

"Aite put this address in your GPS go to that motel. Vinny will meet you in the parking lot and bring you in."

"I got it I'm on my way now." Amir replied hanging up.

Red Bull bared off the Durham exit bumping Ricardo Banks new single Rich World as he drove down the old country road making a right turn he pulled into the trailer park that everyone called Lil Mexico. When he reached the bottom of where the last couple of trailers were located there were a bunch of Mexicans standing outside. Which was not strange but he noticed that there were more than usual, not paying it any mind Red Bull parked the van then slowly got out.

"Hola. How are you doing Torres?"

"Hola señor." Torres chuckled.

"Is everything alright?" Red Bull asked.

"Muy bien."

"Why are all these people here?"

Torres did not answer but continued in Spanish.

"Donde están mis pistolas?" Torres asked.

Red Bull didn't understand what Torres was saying until Torres made a trigger motion with his hand.

"The crates are in the van." Red Bull answered then walked to the back and unlocked the rear door. Torres followed accompanied by five Mexicans trailing behind him. Red Bull lifted the door then Torres motioned for two of the Mexicans to unload the van. Red Bull watches as each crate was unloaded. When Torres people were finished Red Bull turned around expecting payment instead of holding a suitcase Torres held a forty-five in his hand and Red Bull was facing down its barrel.

"Yo what the fuck?" Red Bull hollered surprised.

"King Charles send his regards." Torres said right before he pulled the trigger blowing Red Bulls face off dropping his lifeless body to the ground.

"Pick him up and throw him in the van." Torres instructed his soldiers after Red Bulls body was thrown inside one of the Mexicans got in the driver seat and pulled off.

Pulling into the Motel Six parking lot Amir noticed a tinted blackout Suburban parked down the end of the parking lot. Harlem World drove his Impala closer to the truck then stopped. The driver of the Suburban flicked his lights.

"That's him." Harlem World said.

"Pull up beside him." Amir replied.

When Harlem World pulled up Vinny rolled the window down in his SUV.

"Yo what's up?" Vinny said.

"You must be Vinny?" Amir said.

"Yeah, that's me, and you must be Amir, and you're Harlem World, am I right?" Vinny said with a smirk on his face.

"Yeah, so where are we going?" Amir asked.

"The mansions right up the road not too far from here, follow me."

"Alright lead the way. We're right behind you."

Vinny pulled off with the Impala right behind him following closely. When they reached the mansion Justice was standing outside waiting for them to pull in. Amir and Harlem World were the first to get out.

"Yo what the fuck man this house is big as shit." Amir acknowledged dapping Justice up.

"You got fucking cows out here man." Harlem World added.

"Nice to see both of you. I know the place is a little unusual, but believe me it's new to me too. I see you met Vinny." Justice said.

"Yeah we spoke a few words."

"Good, he's head of security here. I want ya'll to get familiar with each other, but first come inside. I need to let you know what's going on." Justice said turning to walk inside motioning for everyone to follow him.

Once inside Justice led them to the basement where there was nothing but a huge oak table with small oak chairs around it and a huge oak chair that was shaped like a lion's mouth sat at the head of the table. Justice motioned for his three soldiers to take their seats before he sat in the mouth of the lion.

"Earlier today Lisa was attacked by a hit man from Money-B's crew."

"Is she okay?" Harlem World asked.

"Yes she is fine now. If it wasn't for Vinny showing up when he did, she could have been killed."

Hearing what Justice said Harlem World looked at Vinny, and nodded his head in approval Amir did the same.

"Vinny here knew the hitman, and he also knows who has taken over after Money-B." Justice informed.

Amir looked over at Vinny again. "Who's running the show now?" Amir asked.

"Rondo, he was Money-B's general."

"Where do we find this Rondo character, so he can be disposed of?" Harlem World stated.

"I'm not sure, but I know he's in Charlotte. He has to be at Money-B's mansion." Vinny answered.

"How do we find Money-B's mansion?" Amir asked.

"We have to press his people down in Clara Cox maybe one of them can give us a direct address." Vinny explained.

"That sounds like a plan to me." Amir said.

Before Vinny could explain more he felt his phone vibrate. He reached in his pocket and answered it.

"Yo."

"Sir, we have movement about six houses up, two cars are parked on the side of the road."

"I'm on my way up now." Vinny replied before hanging up.

"What's wrong?" Justice asked.

"There's movement, two cars parked close to the mansion. I have to go upstairs, and check it out, will you excuse me?" Vinny said as he stood up from the table.

"I'm going wit you." Harlem World said also standing up.

"Very well, come on." Vinny replied then they both shot up the stairs.

Justice and Amir remained in the basement, and began to put a plan together. After the plan was set Justice told Amir about his family beef with King Charles. Running upstairs Vinny and Harlem World jumped into one of the black bullet proof Suburbans that was parked out front three other soldiers hopped in one of the other SUV's, then they shot down the mansions long driveway. Pulling onto the road with Vinny, and Harlem World in the lead truck. Harlem World pulled one of his Glocks out and checked the clip then slammed it back in and chambered a round readying himself for whatever came his way. While driving Vinny pulled out his walkie talkie and hit the button.

"I'ma ride pass the two cars, ya'll hang back. If I see a threat I'll radio back, over." Vinny said.

"Copy that sir."

Pulling up on the two cars Vinny slowed the SUV down, as he drove pass looking inside the two Crown Vics. The first thing he saw was two people in the backseat with a pair of AKs laying across their laps, Vinny hit the walkie talkie.

"They are armed everything is a go, over."

"Copy that sir, we're engaging now." The soldier said in return mashing the gas speeding the SUV up.

"Yo, you see how that guy was looking at our cars?"

"What guy?" BG asked.

"Whoever was inside that SUV that just rode by."

"Yo you tripping." BG said looking at the remote he held in his hand that showed the camera footage of his drone. "Yo, I gotta bead on Justice, he just came outside he walking with some guy both of them are armed." BG informed he was about to say something else then the screen on the remote went black. "What the fuck." BG hollered frustrated.

"Yo another SUV speeding toward us, I think they've made us."

BG looked and saw what his soldier was speaking of. "Yo get them K's up spray that truck." BG ordered.

His soldier complied leaning out the window and opening fire. The SUV that shot towards them stopped in front of their car and also opened fire, bullets were bouncing off the SUV.

"Yo get the fuck outta here." BG screamed.

His soldier slammed the already running car in drive and did a u-turn in the middle of the road the car behind them did the same. As they shot down the opposite side of the road another black SUV shot in their direction. 'Bloc' 'Bloc' 'Bloc'. The guy in the passenger side of the SUV sent three rounds through the front windshield one of those rounds hit BG in the shoulder "Aaaah." BG hollered feeling the pain of his shoulder burning.

"Get us the fuck outta here." BG screamed looking back in the backseat he saw one of his soldiers had been hit in the head. The car behind them were being chased by the other SUV they were trying to box them in.

"Go around them."

BG's soldier hit the gas driving around the oncoming truck the other car followed suit the oncoming SUV flew past them but still the back car was being chased by the first SUV, until BG looked in the rearview mirror and saw one of his soldiers shoot the front passenger tire out causing the truck to run into a ditch. BG made a mental note to give his goon a raise. Almost in the clear they got on the interstate and shot down the highway.

Vinny and Harlem World watched as the two cars got away. Turning the truck around Vinny pulled up beside the other SUV, so his security team could get inside then they headed back to the mansion. Pulling down the long driveway dust flew everywhere. When the truck stopped the dust cleared. Justice and Amir stood in the front yard Justice had a drone in his hand. Harlem World was the first to hop out the truck.

"Did ya'll get whoever it was?" Justice asked.

"No! They got away, what is that thing in your hand?" Harlem World asked.

"It's a drone. I heard it flying, and shot it down. It had some type of camera on it. Whoever it was were watching us."

"Whoever it was knew that they couldn't get close to this house. It has to be Rondo, I didn't recognize anyone inside the first car but I know it's him." Vinny stated.

"I'm tired of hearing this mutha fuckas name already." Amir said looking at Harlem World.

"Me too bruh." Harlem answered.

"Let's turn the fucking heat up then." Justice said. "I want both of ya'll to rundown and snatch one of them Clara Cox guys up and beat all the information you can out of them, and you keep doing it until you get the information we need to move on Rondo."

"Where is Red Bull?" Justice asked.

"He went on the run to Durham, he should've called me by now tho." Amir said as he reached for his phone and dialed Red Bulls number. 'Ring' 'Ring' 'Ring' 'Ring'. The voicemail then came on.

"He didn't answer, this ain't like Bull. I'ma try this shit again." Amir stated.

'Ring' 'Ring' 'Ring' 'Ring' 'Ring'. Voicemail.

"Shit I got the damn voicemail again. I'ma call my man, and see if he made the drop." Amir said still kinda puzzled because his friend wasn't picking up. He dialed Torres number.

'Ring' 'Ring'.

"Hola (What up homie)." Torres answered.

"Hola bruh. Did my partner make the drop?" Amir asked.

"Yeah he made it, but he's gone."

"What you mean he's gone?" Amir asked not liking the sound of Torres voice.

"He's gone bruh that's all I can say. It was out of my control."

"Who did it? Did you do it mutha fucka, tell me you son of a bitch." Amir screamed.

"King Charles, but you didn't hear it from me sorry bruh it was nothing I could do." Torres replied before hanging up.

After getting off the phone with Torres, Amir broke down.

"What's wrong bruh, what happened?" Justice asked not knowing how to console his friend.

"He's gone bruh, those taco eating mutha fuckas killed him."

"Killed who fam?" Harlem World asked.

"Red Bull."

"What! Shit come on man no no not him." Justice said honestly hurt.

"Who was responsible, was it Torres?" Justice asked.

"No it was King Charles, that's who Torres said it was. I could hear the fear in his voice when he said his name."

Justice was in a state of shock at hearing King Charles name. No one knew they did business with the Mexicans. King Charles reach was longer than he thought, Justice thought to himself.

"Yo let's go inside it's time to close the chapter on these mutha fuckas." Justice stated then they all walked inside.

Chapter 21

Grim Reapers Calling

After getting a disturbing phone call from BG last night letting him know that he had been shot and one of his soldiers was killed when Justice spotted them, he informed Rondo that they barely escaped with their lives. Rondo was furious, that was the last thing that he was trying to hear as he prepared for his meeting with King Charles, this wasn't the time for failure. He needed to get rid of Justice, and he needed to do it fast. Still he hasn't heard from Danger, so he went ahead and crossed him out of his mind truly believing that he was dead. If he wasn't and Danger popped up showing his face, he would definitely kill him. It wasn't a doubt in his mind about that. Snapping himself out of his thoughts, hearing Wendy's voice over the intercom letting him know that there was a man named Rahman out front waiting to see him.

"I'll be right down baby." Rondo replied speaking through the intercom checking his watch he seen that it was 2:30 in the afternoon. Still early he thought to himself as he got up off the couch he looked over at his desk seeing that his forty-five caliber revolver still sit on the table. He thought about grabbing it but later figured that would be a bad idea. After sliding on his flight jacket. Rondo walked downstairs to the kitchen grabbing himself a peach out of Wendy's fruit basket he bit into it tasting its sweetness, as Wendy walked in the kitchen looking sexy as ever.

"Baby, are you okay you don't look like yourself?" Wendy asked.

"Yeah I'm good. I'll see you when I get back." Rondo answered as he walked over and tongue kissed Wendy.

"Where's the guy that came to meet me?"

"I told him to come in, but he said he would wait outside."

"Okay thanks baby." Rondo replied walking out the kitchen and out the front door. When he got outside and saw Rahman sitting on the hood of his Benz butterflies began to flutter in his stomach. He took a deep breath and walked over to Rahman.

"Yo what's up, I'm Rondo." He said trying to introduce himself.

"I know who you are get in the car." Rahman replied letting him know from the door that this wasn't intended to be a friendly meeting. No doubt Rondo did as he was told. Rahman threw the siwak stick he was chewing on the ground and got in the driver side and pulled off. Riding down 85 there was no music being played. Only a lecture by a Muslim scholar warning his listeners about the hell fire. Hearing the scholar made Rondo even more nervous but he put on his best Oscar performance and hid his weak emotions. After a three and a half hour drive that felt like torture they were finally pulling up at King Charles' mansion. Rondo looked around he noticed that the place looked like a fortress, there were people on the roof carrying assault rifles and wearing face paint that made them look like Navy SEALs. When Rahman pulled the Benz up to the carport two armored trucks pulled in behind them and four people got out dressed in army fatigues. Rahman got out and didn't say a word to the soldiers he only pointed at Rondo and in a blink of an eye he was being snatched out of the car.

"Rahman, what's going on?" Rondo hollered as he was being dragged away. Rahman didn't even turn around and acknowledge him he continued walking until he disappeared through a steel door. A bag was thrown over Rondo's head as he was dragged into an empty room, and tied to a chair. The soldiers remained in the room. Rondo listened as he heard the soldiers talking about what they were going to do to him if he made the old man upset.

Rahman walked up the steps feeling no remorse about what may happen to Rondo. Failure wasn't tolerated in their line of work. Either you got the job done or the job killed you end of story. When Rahman reached the top of the steps he opened the door that led to the inside of the mansion. The first person he saw was his brother Ra'mon.

"Is everything taken care of?" Ra'mon asked.

"Of course he's in the quiet room now, where is the old man?"

"He's eating and watching that old movie called Hoodlum about Bumpy Johnson." Ra'mon stated.

"Aite I'ma go let him know that everything is in place." Rahman said.

"Go ahead, if he cusses you out for disturbing him don't blame me." Ra'mon replied chuckling. Rahman didn't say a word, he just walked in King Charles' room, and sat down beside him.

"This steak is wonderful son. You should have to cook make you one." King Charles said as he cut the steak and put a piece in his mouth. "Delicious, you gotta try this." King Charles stated.

"I will when things are settled. Mikal's general is in the quiet room ready for you to speak with him." Rahman informed.

"Good, well let us not keep him waiting." King Charles replied sitting his fork down on the plate. He grabbed his cane that laid on the wall then he stood up and Rahman did the same walking slowly beside him. Ra'mon joined them as they walked to the quiet room. Once inside they walked into a separate room where there was only a single reclining chair facing a huge glass window. King Charles sat down then handed his cane to Ra'mon as both of the boys he raised stood on each side of him.

"Rahman, turn the intercom on for me please." King Charles instructed.

Rahman did as he was told, and walked over to the wall flipping the switch, he returned to King Charles side.

"Take that bag off his face so he can see me." King Charles instructed the two soldiers that stood in the room with Rondo.

When they snatched the bag off his face King Charles could see the fear in his eyes.

"Do you know that when people come to visit me they never leave?" King Charles informed.

"No sir, I didn't know." Rondo answered.

"Do you know that failure is not tolerated here?"

"I am trying my best sir."

"To try is to fail, my orders are what you obey or die there is no other option."

"I understand that sir." Rondo exclaimed clearly terrified.

"I don't believe you do, but I'm sure you will after today if I should allow you to leave. Now tell me why Justice isn't dead?"

"He is hard to locate sir, I've tried everything I've sent my best man at him."

"Do you enjoy taking over after my grandson?"

"No sir, this is not a position I am used to."

"Do you value your life?"

"Yes."

"Then you must value time."

"I do."

"Life is made up of time so it must be cherished as much as you cherish your life. Do you understand this Rondo?"

"I understand sir."

"I don't think you do yet but you will I promise you."

"Beat him until I tell you to stop." King Charles ordered his soldiers.

Hearing the order they began beating Rondo as King Charles, Rahman, and Ra'mon looked on.

"Violence is part of life and it should be remembered, Rondo you sit in my grandsons place a pitiful disgrace. You were his general and you let him die then you come to me with failure. You will kill Justice yourself, do you hear me?" King Charles hollered.

"Stop beating him so he can speak." King Charles said. "Do you hear me Rondo?"

"Yes I hear you." Rondo whispered coughing up blood spitting through his swollen lips.

"Cut him loose." King Charles ordered then he watched as his soldiers cut him loose.

"Stand the fuck up, I wanna see if you have some heart."

Rondo wiped his face with the sleeve his eyes were swollen and his face was badly beaten but he slowly stood to his feet.

"Fight them! I want to see what Mikal seen in you."

Rondo threw up his guard and lunged at one of the soldiers who side stepped his swing and pushed him to the ground. Rondo stood back up the second soldier kicked knocking the wind out of him but he caught the soldier's foot and with all his strength he slung him to the ground. Falling on top of him Rondo grabbed the soldiers knife then stood over the soldier with the knife at his throat the other soldier tried to help him, but King Charles gave the order for him to not move.

"If you spend too much time thinking you'll never get it done, kill him." King Charles ordered. Without a second though Rondo slit his throat then he stood up with the dead soldier's knife still in his hand.

"You will kill or you will be killed there is no in between. You have bought yourself another twenty four hours. I expect Justice to be dead before that time is up. If not my son will be paying you another visit. You are free to leave our meeting is over."

"How am I supposed to get back?" Rondo asked.

"One of the soldiers will give you a car. You were lucky today no one ever leaves this place alive. I suggest you do not let the old man down. If you do your death will be very painful." Ra'mon replied answering rondo's question knowing that King Charles was done talking to him. Rondo nodded his head then watched the old man walk out of the room. The young soldier that stood beside him grabbed him by the collar and pushed him out of the quiet room leaving the dead soldier on the floor.

As Agent Slade pulled into Butner Federal Penitentiary all he could think about was Justice and finding a way to stop this family war. Too many people have been killed because of the Santiago and the Sanderson feud for power. After checking his gun in Agent Slade walked inside the facility to the reception desk.

"Hello, I'm Agent Jacobe Slade. I need to see a inmate by the name Christopher Perry." Agent Slade said flashing his federal badge.

"Okay sir walk through these double doors. I'ma buzz you in." the receptionist said.

"Thank you."

After walking through the double doors and being buzzed in he walked into the visitation room then the intercom came on.

"Agent Slade I'm having Perry brought up now. It's count time. Make yourself comfortable he should be up in the next 30 minutes."

"Alright thank you." Agent Slade replied pulling up a seat at one of the empty tables. After about a forty five minute wait the door buzzed and Christopher Perry walked inside and to the table joining the special agent.

"I told you the last time you were here that I wasn't helping you."

"I know what you said, but things are different now."

"What do you mean by that?" Christopher asked.

"Sit down and I'll tell you."

Chris took a deep breath not knowing what the agent was about to say. Everything in him told him to turn around and walk out, but against his better judgement he sat down curious about what the agent had to say.

"I'm listening." Chriss said after sitting down.

"A couple of days ago a guy named Deion Harper was murdered in front of his girlfriend. Someone hunted him down, found him then forced his way into the apartment that him and his girlfriend lived in. The intruder kidnapped the girl and waited til Deion came home. When he did the intruder questioned him and then killed him."

"Okay so what does that have to do with me?" Christopher asked.

"The guy was a professional, he let the girl live. Would you like to know what he wanted?"

"What." Christopher was curious.

"He wanted to know where he could find your son, Justice."

"What do you mean?"

"What I mean is, what I mean is your son is in trouble. I know you already heard about what happened to Kanden Santiago?"

"Yes I've heard."

"I need your help Chris, I believe your son is the head of the family now. I went to see your mother-in-law but of course I got no help there. I need you Chris, your son needs you."

"Vidah." Chris sighed. "That old woman would die before she helped you."

"I know, that's why I need you to help me end this war Chris."

"I told you Slade, I'm not rolling over on my son. It's bad enough that I haven't been in his life."

"You don't have to roll over on him, at least give me something, anything that will help me."

"Okay, I'll give you something on King Charles. I know it was him that had Kanden killed."

"What can you give me?"

"Charles has a warehouse in Charlotte, where he stashes his dirty money inside his expensive cars there should be drugs and guns there to. Charles is old school all the cars are in his name."

"How do you know this?"

"The stuff in the warehouse is Charles' get away stash for if he ever had to go on the run. Me and my wife, we were going to hit that spot after we had a couple soldiers raid his mansion in Atlanta. Unfortunately you locked us up before we could make good on our plan."

"Do you think that stuff is still there?"

"I know it is like I said he's old school and old people don't like changes, you know me telling you this can get me killed."

"I can have you taken to protective custody."

Chris chuckled. "Not in this lifetime, I've done a lot of bad things in my life but the one thing I've never done was run from them. I gave you that information to save my son's life."

"I'll try my best I promise I'll do what I can."

"For his sake I hope you do, but I won't be alive to see it. I'll tell you this if you can bring Charles down then the war would end." Chris replied right before calling for the guards to take him back to his cell.

Back at the Burlington mansion Justice, Harlem World, and Vinny sat inside trying to figure out their next move. Amir was too angry to think clearly saddened by the death of his friend. Justice had already given the order to kidnap and torture. Pressure had to be applied in order to get the information they needed if they didn't they would be sitting ducks fighting a blind war. After everyone came to an agreement Amir, Harlem World, and Vinny left to put their plan into motion.

Feeling a little worn out by all the events that had taken place Justice went upstairs to check on Lisa. When he walked into the bedroom expecting Lisa to be asleep he was surprised to see that she was fully dressed.

"Baby, is everything okay? Why aren't you resting?" Justice inquired.

"I'm good, but I can't sleep. I heard the gunshots outside." Lisa answered.

"That was me having a lil target practice."

"Justice we are better than this. You don't have to lie to me. I know you're trying to protect me but I just killed a man. I'ma big girl I can handle it."

"I'm sure you can. I'm sorry baby I just don't want you involved."

"I'm already involved whether you know it or not. We're family Justice. I love you more than anything in this world."

"I love you too." Justice whispered in Lisa's ear as he hugged her.

"I've been trying to call Maleekah but for some reason she's not answering. Has Amir spoken to her?"

"I don't think so a lot has been going on, so I'm really not sure."

"I had Richard do a background check like you asked. I'll call him later today. It's strange tho I told her we were moving then all of a sudden some guy comes in our house and tries to kill me."

"Did she know where we lived?"

"Yeah I told her. I didn't think it was a secret."

"Did you tell anyone that we were moving here?"

"Yeah, I told her we were moving to Burlington, but not to this place. I didn't know where this place was."

"From now on don't tell nobody anything. I want you to get on the phone and call Richard right now, I wanta know everything about that woman."

"Okay baby don't be mad at me."

"I'm not Lisa. I'm just a lil stressed out is all." Justice said falling back on the king size bed and closing his eyes.

Lisa walked over and kissed him on the forehead before heading downstairs. After Lisa left 30 minutes later Justice phone rang.

"Hello." Justice answered.

"You have a collect call from Butner Federal Correction Facility. You will not be charged for this call. Press five to accept."

Justice didn't hear the name of who was calling but he answered it anyway.

"Yo, who is this?"

"This is your father."

"What, how the fuck did you get this number?" Justice asked in an angry tone.

"I've always had it."

"What do you want? What you need money or something?"

"No son I just wanted to hear your voice that's all."

"If you've always had my number why didn't you call?"

"Because of where I am I was ashamed. Also I promised Vidah I would stay away."

"My grandmother?"

"Yes I wanted her to raise you right so you wouldn't grow up and become like me and your mother."

"Well that didn't happen."

"I know son, well I don't have long. I just wanted to tell you. I love you, and to be careful. There's a F.B.I. agent named Jacobe Slade asking a lot of questions about you don't trust him for nothing okay, he's the one that took your mother down."

"I don't fuck wit the police period, so you don't have to worry about that." Justice answered. 'You have sixty seconds left.'

"The phones about to hang up you take care of yourself okay be better than me and your mother. I love you son, I always have."

"Okay man love you too. Keep in touch." Justice replied and then the phone hung up. Justice sat the phone on the bed then drifted off.

Chapter 22

Pain

After Rondo's horrible experience meeting with King Charles and barely escaping with his life he remembered how dangerous Money-B used to tell him that his grandfather was. Now he knew first hand. He could not let the old man down, he would surely pay with his life if he did. Getting out of the old Chevy pick-up truck that King Charles' soldier had given him to drive home he walked into his mansion and was greeted by Wendy's open arms.

"Baby what happened to you. Are you okay?" Wendy said.

"I'm fine." Rondo replied while Wendy wiped his face.

"You don't look like it, let me go to the kitchen and get you a ice pack." Wendy said after kissing Rondo on the cheek then disappearing into the kitchen.

Rondo walked upstairs to his office and sat behind his desk. Rubbing his temple he thought of the twenty-four hours that

King Charles had given him to kill Justice. He needed to figure out the right course of action and he needed to do it fast. Not too sure of himself he picked up the phone and called Maleekah.

'Ring' 'Ring' 'Ring'.

"Hey baby!" Maleekah answered.

"Hey what's good?"

"Not too much just chillen."

"Are you still in Chapel Hill?"

"No baby you told me to disappear. I'm back at home I'm in Charlotte."

"Look there a change of plan. Have you still been in contact with Justice's girl?"

"No, but she's been calling me all day."

"Okay call her back see if you can get her to meet you somewhere. I'ma have one of my guys snatch her."

"Rondo you know I don't be into the criminal side of the life you're into."

"I know that Maleekah but I need you to do this for me this time. I'll pay double."

"If you're talking about doubling my fee I'm down I'll do this one time. I'm not doing this again Rondo, I'm not trying to go back to jail."

"You're not going to jail. I have everything under control."

"You better, I'll text you when she's with me."

"Thanks baby."

"Yeah just make sure you have my money."

"Don't I always?"

"Yeah, talk to you later." Maleekah said and then hung up.

After talking with Maleekah, Rondo felt a lil bit better. He'd have B.G. kidnap the girl and make Justice come to him the same as he did Money-B. Interrupting his thoughts Wendy's sexy ass walked into his office carrying an ice pack and glass of cold water.

"Here you go baby drink this and take these pills then put this ice pack on your head."

"You know I don't take pills, what kind are they?"

"Aspirin silly." Wendy replied then watched as Rondo took the pill and swallowed them then chased the water down behind it then he laid back in his office chair and put the ice pack over his swollen face.

"Just relax baby, momma going to give you something to relieve your stress." Wendy said as she began to rub on Rondo's thigh until she saw his erection poking through his jeans. Slowly she unbuttoned his jeans and unzipped his fly. Wendy then pulled his seven inch dick out. He wasn't as big as Money-B, but she still enjoyed his sex game. Wendy spit inside her palm then she began to lightly stroke Rondo's dick making his dick get even harder. When she was satisfied knowing that he was at his full length she got down on her knees and slowly inserted his dick in her mouth. Sucking him slowly making love to his dick with her mouth while she looked up staring into his eyes. When he finally came she swallowed every drop of his milky semen.

"Damn babe what's got into you?"

"I wanted to help you relax." Wendy replied wiping her mouth.

Walking downstairs Lisa turned on the T.V. then called her boss Richard Murray at his law firm.

'Ring' 'Ring' 'Ring'.

"Richard Murray and Associates, how may I help you?"

"Richard, this is Lisa."

"Lisa, hey how are you doing?"

"I'm fine."

"I'm glad, I was kinda worried since you didn't call in."

"Family emergency I apologize for not calling."

"It's okay, take your time. I'll hold the fort down while you're away."

"Thanks Richard."

"No problem."

"Did you do that background check that I asked you about?"

"Yeah I did hold up let me go get my notes." Richard replied then walked to his back office.

"Hello." Richard said returning to the phone.

"Yeah."

"Okay let me see here, Maleekah Rainey. She's a native of Charlotte did five years in prison for conspiracy to commit arm robbery."

"Did she have any co-defedents?" Lisa inquired.

"Yeah a guy named Rondo Jefferies, it seems like he didn't do any time tho. Maleekah must have taken all the charges."

"Is that everything?"

"Yeah that's all I could dig up on short notice."

"Thanks Richard, you're a life saver."

"No problem you're welcome Lisa." Richard replied before hanging up.

Justice had awakened from his nap and walked downstairs. The first thing he saw was the shocking look on Lisa's face.

"What's wrong bae? You look like you seen a ghost or something."

"I was just talking with my boss, he did the background check on Maleekah."

"What he say?"

"She has a record, did five years for conspiracy to commit armed robbery. She lives in Charlotte. She had a co-defendant named Rondo Jefferies."

"What the fuck did you just say? Her co-defendant say his name again."

"Rondo Jefferies, baby do you know him or something?"

"Personally, no, but he's the one that's been trying to kill us. I want you to get Maleekah on the phone."

"I've been trying to call her all day, but she hasn't been answering."

"Keep calling her til she picks up. When she does have her meet you at La Cocina the Mexican restaurant on South Church Street, she's the missing piece to the puzzle baby."

"Alright I'ma call her now." Lisa said then she began to dial Maleekah's number.

'Ring' 'Ring' 'Ring'.

"Lisa, hey girl." Maleekah answered.

"Hey Maleekah I've been trying to call you all day."

"My phone must have been off, my bad girl, what's up tho?"

"Nothing really, I was trying to see if you wanted to have a girl's night out. Justice has been getting on my nerves all day."

"Sure what did you have in mind?"

"There's a Mexican restaurant in Burlington called La Cocina they have the best margaritas in town. I thought it would be nice to get a couple of drinks and eat some Mexican food."

"Sounds like a plan, what time do you want to meet up?"

Justice held up nine fingers.

"How about nine o'clock, how does that sound?" Lisa asked.

"Sounds good to me, you wanta drive or do you want me to pick you up?"

"I'll meet you there."

"Alright text me the address."

"I will."

"Talk to you later then." Maleekah said before hanging up.

"What now?" Lisa said to Justice.

"You meet her at the restaurant, Vinny and Harlem World will grab her. Then make her tell us where we can find Rondo."

"I'ma kill that bitch if she's behind all this bullshit."

"Don't worry about her." Justice replied pulling his phone from his pocket he called Amir to put his plan together.

After hanging up with Lisa Maleekah called Rondo back.

'Ring' 'Ring'.

"Yeah." Rondo answered.

"Justice girl just called me."

"That was fast, what's the deal?"

"She wants to have a girl's night out."

"Where at?"

"A restaurant in Burlington on South Church Street. The place is called La Cocina she wants to meet at 9:00pm, what do you want me to do?"

"Go have fun. I'll handle the rest."

"Okay make sure you have my money when this is over."

"I told you I got you." Rondo replied hanging up then immediately calling BG.

After Agent Slade's visit with Christopher Perry he called a fellow agent by the name of Tommy Ray and relayed the information that he had gotten from Chris. Being that he knew that he couldn't get a warrant, he needed back up before he went to check King Charles warehouse out so he had brought Tommy in. Currently heading to Charlotte Agent Slade stopped at a gas station.

"You pump I'll go pay. I gotta use the bathroom any way." Agent Ray said as he got out of Agent Slade's truck and walked inside.

"Don't catch butterflies now." Agent Slade replied.

"Never that." Agent Ray shot back then continued his stride. After paying for the gas Agent Ray walked to the bathroom pulling out his phone he called King Charles.

'Ring' 'Ring'.

"Tommy how you doing?" King Charles said answering his phone.

"We have a problem."

"Talk to me."

"Agent Slade went to see Christopher Perry, he gave you up we're headed to your warehouse now."

"That snitch mutha fucka. Do ya'll have a warrant?"

"No, it's just me and him."

"I want you to take care of it, get rid of him."

"That won't be easy."

"Get it done that's what I pay you for. I'll take care of Chris' snitching ass."

"You're not paying me for this. Do I need to remind you of that?"

"You don't need to remind me of shit just do it. I'll have Ra'mon transfer a million to your off shore account."

"Consider it done." Agent Ray said before hanging up. Then he placed his phone back inside his coat pocket then walked back to the truck and got inside.

"You good?" Agent Slade asked after Agent Ray closed the passenger door.

"Couldn't be better, let's get this done, so we nail this old sonofabitch."

Hearing that Agent Slade smiled then threw the truck in drive and pulled off. After a 20 minute drive both agents pulled into what looked like an abandoned warehouse they got out and check the doors, but they were locked. Looking up Agent Ray saw an opened window.

"Look up there the windows open. I'ma climb inside and open this door and let you in."

"Aite I'll be right here."

Agent Ray climb up the ladder leading to the open window. Once he was at the top he climb inside the window and jumped down then walked to the door and unlocked it letting Agent Slade inside.

"Damn." Agent Slade said as he seen the four S500 Benz's.

"We gotta search these cars." Agent Slade said pulling out his service Glock and shooting off the trunk locks. He returned his pistol to his holster and proceeded to search the trunks Agent Ray did the same. The trunks were full of guns and money and a book bag with tapes and notebooks were inside each car.

"We gotta call this in." Agent Slade said.

"I'm afraid, I can't let you do that." Agent Ray replied.

Hearing that Agent Slade turned around and found himself facing down the barrel of an M-16.

"What the fuck Tommy? Don't tell me King Charles has gotten to you too?"

"I'm afraid so Slade it's not personal it's just business."

"Business, you're a fucking federal agent Tommy. Whatever Charles has on you we can get through it together. I'll help you."

"It's not that easy Slade. You should've never came back."

On instinct Agent Slade went for his gun Agent Ray pulled the trigger instantly killing Agent Slade. Then he wiped the gun off making sure it was clean and had no finger prints. He threw the assault rifle back in the trunk then pulled out his phone and called King Charles.

'Ring'.

"Yeah." King Charles answered.

"It's done."

"Good job Tommy you're a million dollars richer."

"He's in the warehouse."

"Leave him, I'll have someone come and clean the place."

"How do you expect me to leave?"

"Walk to the car rental place down the street there's a car waiting it's already been arranged black Honda Accord the keys are under the mat." King Charles instructed.

"What about his truck, it's outside?"

"What I say, you know I don't like repeating myself. Don't worry about it just leave."

"Okay." Agent Ray replied before hanging up then he walked out of the warehouse and didn't look back thinking about the trip he would take with his wife.

9:00pm Amir and Harlem World had gotten the call from Justice about Maleekah, and the plan to grab her. Amir pulled behind La Cocina after watching Lisa park in the front of the restaurant and walked inside. Amir had let Vinny out of the van down the street so he could radio them if he noticed that Maleekah was being tailed. When they were stationed Harlem World and Amir got out and posted up by the back door of the kitchen. Harlem World went inside once he walked through the kitchen and walked around the bar. He peeked inside the sitting area to make sure Lisa was sitting in the back booth as planned then he slowly slid in the girls bathroom into an empty stall and waited.

Maleekah pulled into the restaurants parking lot checking her watch it was 9:10pm, she got out of her car and looked around until she seen a couple of Rondo's men that had followed. Deep down she was kinda shaky and didn't want to go through with Rondo's plan but she felt like she didn't have a choice. Secretly she loved Rondo and would do anything for him and the fact that he was doubling her pay gave her the motivation that she needed. Grabbing her purse and shutting the door Maleekah walked inside.

Lisa sat in the last stall farthest to the back with her nine inside her purse. She smiled from ear to ear as she saw Maleekah walk through the door.

"Hey girl." Lisa said.

"Hey." Maleekah replied, as she walked over and hugged Lisa.

"How have you been?" Lisa asked after both girls sat down.

"Busy working."

"You like the bartending job?"

"Yeah, it's okay it's not what I really wanta do tho. But it's okay for now."

As they both sat and chit chat the waitress walked up.

"May I take your order?" the waitress asked.

"Sure, uh let's get a pitcher of margarita lime and let me get a order of chicken wings and fries."

"And you ma'am, what would you like?" the waitress asked turning to Maleekah.

"I'll have the same." Maleekah answered.

"Alright, I'll be right back." The waitress said before walking off to fill their orders both girls continued their girl talk until they were interrupted as the waitress came back with their pitcher of margaritas lime and their salted glasses. She neatly sat them on the table.

"Thank you."

"You're welcome, your food will be out in a few minutes." The waitress said before leaving again Lisa grabbed the pitcher and filled both of their glasses, Maleekah took the first sip.

"Girl this is good, this just might be the best margarita in town."

"Trust me it is take your time it'll hit you fast too." Lisa warned.

Maleekah smiled and downed her first glass. After the second she was feeling rather tipsy and realized she had drunk more than she had planned.

"Lisa let me go to the bathroom. I have to pee like a race horse." Maleekah said as she got up and walked to the ladies room.

Instantly Lisa flipped herself into gear readying herself for what was about to take place, she watched as Maleekah disappeared into the restroom.

After sitting in the stall for what felt like hours, but was really around thirty minutes. Harlem World heard the door open and a female come sit in the stall next to him. He listened as she used the bathroom, slowly he pulled his Glock out and sat it on his lap. After the woman was finished relieving herself he peeked through the crack in the stalls door and watched as the woman washed her hands. He couldn't front the girl was sexy as hell and he was kinda feeling her but he had a job to do. Pushing his lustful thoughts out of his head he slung the stall door open and pointed his Glock at the back of Maleekah's head. She was terrified tears began to run down the girls face. "Don't make a sound. If you do I'll be forced to kill you. We're going to walk outta here through the kitchen and out the back door." Just as Harlem World was about to continue his instructions his phone vibrated. A text came thru it was Amir telling him that Vinny had spotted Maleekah's tail and was moving in on them. After looking at the text he returned his phone to his pocket.

"You think you're a slick bitch huh?"

"What are you talking about?"

"The people that followed you here." Harlem World replied pushing the Glock's barrel to the back of her head.

"No one followed me. I don't know what you're talking about?" Maleekah shot back.

"It doesn't matter now, come on let's go." Harlem World said grabbing the back of her neck he lowered his Glock down to the middle of Maleekah's back and lightly pushed her out of the bathroom door.

When they walked out the first person Maleekah saw was Lisa, to her surprise she wasn't sitting in the booth where she left her. She was standing by the bathroom door smiling at her.

"Yeah, you tried it, but it didn't work." Lisa said then she followed Harlem World around the bar and through the kitchen and out the back door. Amir grabbed Maleekah and tied her up and threw her in the back of the van. Lisa and Harlem World jumped in the back with her, and Amir got in the driver side.

Vinny was trained to spot certain things, being in the military he had learned every form of killing and the ability to spot an enemy from far away. It was often hard in Iraq spotting children, and women that had bombs strapped to them underneath their clothing, but he did it and he did it well, so spotting a tail was very easy for him. He considered killing the two guys that had followed the woman, but they were at a public place. Killing them would certainly draw a scene. He had radioed Amir and let him know that the woman had been followed. Sitting across the street he spotted the black work van come from behind the restaurant. They must have grabbed the girl to not have had any training those boys were good Vinny thought to himself, as he watched the van pull right up in front of him. The side door slid open and he jumped inside with Lisa, Harlem World, and a tied up and gagged Maleekah, Amir pulled off. Heading to an abandoned trailer on Apple Street. When they arrived they ushered Maleekah inside, Lisa threw her on the floor and began kicking her in the face with her heels. Amir walked over and pulled her off of Maleekah.

"Stop sis before you kill her, calm down."

"Fuck that bitch. She's been trying to set us up."

"I know just calm down at least let me get what I need out of her then you can do whatever you want to her." Amir whispered in her ear then he let her go.

"Fine, hurry up." Lisa replied then she went and stood in the corner gripping her purse. Harlem World walked over to Maleekah and picked her up off the floor and sat her in an old dirty pissy couch then he snatched her gag off.

"Now tell me where can I find Rondo?" Harlem World asked.

"I don't know who you are talking about." Maleekah replied.

"Of course you do, he's your boyfriend or either you're working for him. Which one is it?" Harlem World stated.

"I don't know him."

"Okay have it your way." Harlem World pulling a pair of steel pliers from his pocket. "I suggest you stop lying to us and tell my friend here what he wants to know. You're a fine woman I was really feeling you. I would hate to have him mess up your pretty face." Amir informed.

"I don't know him Amir. I promise you." Maleekah pleaded.

"Okay have it your way you can't say I didn't try. Harlem, Vinny do what you do." Amir said looking on Harlem World smiled knowing exactly what he was about to do. He told Vinny to untie her and hold her down. When Vinny had her in place Harlem World walked over and grabbed Maleekah's left hand. He took the steel pliers and peeled Maleekah's pinky finger nail off then he grabbed her ring finger and did the same peeling the nail off. Maleekah's screams were deafening they all watched as Maleekah pass out from the pain. Minutes later she was awakened again by a splash of water hitting her face.

"Now tell me where I can find Rondo?" Amir asked a dizzy Maleekah as expected Maleekah mumbled the address. Amir smiled to himself satisfied with his slight victory.

"She's all yours Lisa." Amir stated.

"My pleasure." Lisa replied pulling her Glock from her purse she shot Maleekah in the face spraying her brains on the floor then she passed her Glock to a startled Amir.

"Get rid of that for me please." Lisa said.

"That's not a problem, but damn sis where that come from. I thought you were going to whoop her ass some more. You went and killed the girl."

"We don't have time to be playing let's get outta here." Lisa stated then she walked out of the abandoned trailer with Vinny following behind her.

"See, now I'm starting to like her." Harlem World said.

"I know right let's get outta here." Amir replied as they both walked out.

Around 11:30pm Rondo had gotten a call from BG letting him know that they had lost Maleekah. He was furious and couldn't truly understand how that was possible, they were supposed to snatch Justices girl, but instead Maleekah somehow up and dis-

appeared in thin air. BG had explained that both girls went inside but they never came out and when it had gotten too late they went inside the restaurant but they both were gone. They had questioned the waitress, but she had acted like the two women never came inside. After hanging up Rondo didn't know what to do. What he did know was that his life was on the clock, and right now he was in a fucked up position. The only thing that worried him was the information that she may have given up if Justice had applied the right pressure.

Back at Justice's mansion Amir broke down the events that happened and gave Justice the information that he had gathered from Maleekah. He also informed him of Lisa's actions which surprised Justice more than anything and the fact that she didn't say a word to him about it bothered him even more. For some reason he had felt coldness in her when she walked in the house. He had known something wasn't right but he couldn't quite put his finger on it. He took a mental note to speak with her about it later. After going over the details Justice, Amir, Vinny, and Harlem World sat down and began putting a plan together to take Rondo out. They stayed up til three in the morning before all four of them agreed on the right course of action. When everything was certain and the plan was set, only then did they fall asleep.

The next day shit was up and poppin. Vinny and a few of his soldier headed to Charlotte to one of Justices newly owned cable business where they met up with one of Justice's old friends named Hawk. Once they were at the cable company Hawk had given them a device that could scramble phone and cable frequencies which would in turn make any cameras that were set up useless and would require a manual restart. During their planning last night Vinny had informed Justice that since Rondo had just taken over for Money-B he didn't have the time to figure out which business Justice now owned so if they blocked his system out it would be a strong chance that he would call Justice's company for repairs and instead of sending company men he could send a few of his soldiers in dressed as company men.

After Hawk showed Vinny how to work the device, as usuall he collected his money and went on his way. Vinny showed his top soldier how to work the device then he sent him to Rondo's address to work his magic.

Rondo woke up naked in the bed beside Wendy with nothing but murder on his mind. He had a mission to complete and he had to have it done by the end of the day or he was a dead man walking. After the wild sex that he had with Wendy last night he was still kinda exhausted but he paid his tiredness no mind. Instead he took himself a cold shower. When he got out and got dressed he turned on the news and picked up his phone and called BG during the middle of their conversation the phone went dead and the cable on the T.V. went out.

"What the fuck." Rondo hollered in frustration then he picked up his cell phone and tried to call BG Back, but all he got was the dial tone. "What the fuck is going on?" Rondo thought to himself.

"Wendy." Rondo hollered.

"Yeah."

"Call the electrician & cable company something wrong with the T.V."

"Which one you want me to call?"

"Can Valley Cable & Electric get their guys out here?"

"Okay baby I'm calling now."

Sitting in the office Vinny waited patiently for the phone to ring. Valley Cable & Electric had the best service in the city. The company stayed busy around the clock, so it was no doubt that they would get a call from Rondo's address. After waiting for what seemed like hours the phone finally rang.

"Hello Valley Cable & Electric. How may I help you today?" Vinny asked.

"My name is Wendy. We're having problems with our cable and our telephone."

"What type of problem are you having ma'am?"

"I don't know really the cable has gone out and the phones and the cameras are blinking on and off."

"Okay I'll send a service vehicle out to you. I'll need your address."

"It should already be logged into your system under the name Mikal Sanderson."

Vinny heard the name and was shocked he really couldn't believe his plan was working. He typed the name in the computer and the address popped right up.

"Alright ma'am, I see your address on the screen. I'll send someone right out."

"Thank you very much."

"You're welcome it's a pleasure doing business with you." Vinny replied before hanging up.

"Yo we gotta hit suit up." Vinny said to his three soldiers.

Hearing the command all three guys put on Valley Cable & Electric uniforms they checked their pistols and made sure their silencers were in their tool boxes then they loaded up in two separate company vans two people in each unit. They crunk up and headed to the address with Vinny in the lead on the way there Vinny had called Justice.

"Hello." Justice answered.

"We're on our way to Rondo now."

"Good, text me the address."

"I will, what is the order? What do you want us to do once we're inside?"

"Secure everyone and then call me. Me and my Stunna Boys will be on the way as soon as you text me the location."

"So you don't want us to kill him?"

"No, I want to speak with him first he might can tell me something about King Charles."

"Okay, I gotcha boss. I'm texting the info now. You got it?"

"Yeah."

"I'll call when we're inside." Vinny said before hanging up.

After a twenty minute drive Vinny and his crew pulled up to the gate of Rondo's mansion. They were stopped by two security guards.

"Hold sir we have to have confirmation before you enter." The security guard said.

"A lady name Wendy called and requested service." Vinny replied.

"We're checking on it now." The security guard replied then said a few words into his walkie talkie and then waited for a response. Vinny could hear an angry man's voice come over the air waves. Gripping his Beretta 9 tightly that he had hidden in his lap.

"Is everything okay?" Vinny asked.

"Yeah, you've been cleared. We have to check the back of the van first then you can go through."

"Okay sir the doors unlocked." Vinny replied then he watched as one guard opened the back of his van and the other guard walked and checked the back of the second van. When both vans had been cleared both security guards walked back to their post and opened the gate. Instead of going right through Vinny got out of the van hiding his Beretta 9 behind his back with a clipboard in his hand.

"Excuse me sir, I need for one of you to sign this sheet. It's the only way we can get paid." Vinny said handing the clipboard to one of the guards.

"Give it here." The guard demanded snatching the clip board from Vinny. Once the clipboard was out of Vinny's hand he pulled the Beretta 9 from behind his back and then shot the first then the second guard in the face dropping them instantly. Vinny bent down and picked up the bloody clip board as two of his soldiers quickly got out of the vans and dragged both security guards bodies inside the guard house and covered them up. Returning to their vans Vinny led them through the gate.

Pulling up in the front of the huge mansion Vinny was taken aback by the fact that the place wasn't nearly as guarded as his previous bosses was. Vinny and his solders got out of the van and retrieved their toolboxes. Vinny went to knock on the door, but a slim woman had already opened it and was standing in the door way dressed in an all white pant suit that showed her cleavage.

Vinny swallowed. "Huh we're here to fix your system."

"I figured that much, sorry about the hassle at the gate."

"It's okay ma'am it's part of the business."

"Well my name is Wendy, I'm the one that called you. Why don't you come in I'll show you to the box inside."

"Okay, but my other two guys need to check the boxes around the house. Me and my partner can check the one inside." Vinny answered.

"Okay well you know how to do your job."

Vinny laughed then ordered the two soldiers to check the boxes outside before he walked inside following behind Wendy. Vinny couldn't front Wendy was sexy as hell and he hated to do what he was about to do. After Wendy led them to the fuse box that was located in the kitchen. He opened it and began to mess with the breakers.

"Ma'am, when we begin working all the T.V.s must be cut off and no one on the phone." Vinny instructed.

"You don't have to worry about that, no one else is here but my boyfriend and he's in his office he won't be any trouble." Wendy answered honestly.

Hearing that Vinny reached inside his toolbox while doing so he gave his partner a look that only he knew what it meant. His soldier went into immediate action. Pulling his gun from inside his coat grabbing Wendy from behind with his hand pressed over her mouth. Vinny stood up and screwed the silencer on his Beretta 9.

"I don't wanna hurt you, but I need you to tell me where Rondo is, matter of fact I need for you to show me. Nod your head if you understand." Vinny demanded.

Wendy slowly nodded her head. Seeing that she understood Vinny pulled a set of zip ties from his pocket.

"I'ma put these around your wrists. Like I said we do not want to hurt you but if you make a sound when he removes his hand from your face I'm going to kill you, slowly nod your head if you're with me."

Wendy nodded.

"Take your hand off her face and tie her hand with these." Vinny instructed as he handed the zip ties to his soldier and watched as he removed his hand from her face and began to tie her hands together.

"I'm glad you know how to follow instructions."

"What do you want?" Wendy whispered.

"All we want is Rondo I assure you, now take me to him."

"He's in his office."

"Show me." Vinny replied grabbing Wendy by the back of her neck. He pushed her out of the kitchen and followed her closely as she led the way.

When they got to the top of the stairs, Wendy led them to a room with two huge double doors. "He's in there." Wendy whispered.

"Open the door." Vinny commanded.

"It's hard with my hands tied behind my back."

Vinny looked at his soldier without a word being said between them. The soldier grabbed Wendy by the back of her neck and the small of her back, he lifted her off her feet and threw her through the double doors. Wendy screamed as her face hit the door and she went flying into Rondo's office falling on the floor. "What the fuck." Rondo hollered as he slid his chair away from his office desk.

"Don't fucking move bitch." Vinny ordered as he walked inside Rondo's office with his Beretta 9 pointed at his skull.

"Restrain him." Vinny ordered his partner.

"Who the fuck sent you here, my twenty four hours isn't up." Rondo pleaded.

"Shut the fuck up." Vinny's soldier ordered as he punched him in the face making Rondo fall out of his office chair then he began to stomp him in the face.

"Tie him up, Justice doesn't want him killed. He wants to speak with him first." Vinny uttered. The soldier complied pulling out a set of zip ties, he tied Rondo's hands together.

Vinny pulled out his walkie talkie.

"The package is secured." Vinny radioed his other two soldiers outside.

"Outside perimeter is secured, what are the orders?"

"Guard the place I'm calling Justice."

"Ten fo over."

Vinny returned his walkie talkie to his pocket then he pulled out his phone and called Justice.

'Ring' 'Ring'.

"Yo." Justice answered.

"I have the package the place is secured two of our boys are outside manning the perimeter."

"Good job Vinny we're twenty minutes out."

"Thank you sir. We'll be here waiting." Vinny replied before hanging up.

Chapter 23

Invincible

"We're twenty minutes out, Vinny and his team has already secured the area." Justice said.

"I can't wait to see this fuck boys face when he finally sees us." Amir replied.

"Yeah I'ma carve a pretty little smile on his face." Harlem World uttered from the back seat.

"Not before I get all of the information that I need outta him. After that he's all yours."

"Yeah then we'll have some real fun." Harlem World whispered as he sat back in his seat and enjoyed the rest of the ride.

20 minutes later

"Lock and load we're here boys." Justice voiced as he pulled his Suburban up to the gate. Slowly he rolled down the window and noticed that he was speaking to one of Vinny's men.

"Everything's good sir, Vinny is waiting on you."

Justice looked down and spotted the legs of one of the dead guards laying on the ground.

"Good job soldier." Justice replied.

"Thank you sir." The soldier returned his gratitude as he pushed the button opening the gate to let his boss through.

Justice pulled down further into the estate until he was directly in front of the mansion. He parked right behind the two Valley Cable & Electric vans and they all got out of the SUV. Justice pulled out his phone and called Vinny.

Ring, Ring.

"Sir." Vinny answered.

"I'm here at the front door."

"I'm sending my partner down now." Vinny replied and then hung up and looked to his partner.

"Go let them in." Vinny commanded.

"Yes sir." He said then disappeared.

Justice, Amir, and Harlem World stood outside gripping their AR-15 assault rifles ready to dead any outsider. The front door opened, Justice looked at his soldier and smiled.

"Take me to Rondo."

"Follow me right this way sir."

Justice and his Stunna Boys followed him as he led the way upstairs and into Rondo's office. When the three walked inside the first person Justice and Harlem World noticed was Vinny pointing his gun at a tied up light skin guy. Seeing this Harlem World ran up to Rondo and smacked the shit outta him knocking him to the ground then he pulled Rondo by the collar and punched him in the face.

"That's enough Harlem you'll have plenty of time for that." Justice said as he walked up to Vinny and patted him on the shoulder then he bent down until he was looking Rondo directly in his eyes.

"So you are the one who has been causing me so much trouble?" Justice stated.

"Fuck you." Rondo said spitting blood on the floor.

"Damn, you don't have to be so aggressive. I was impressed with the play you did with the girl, of course you know that she's dead.

Rondo didn't say a word he just dropped his head.

"What I want to know is more about King Charles, I want you to tell me how I can find him."

"If I tell you that he'll kill me."

Justice stood up. "What do you suppose I'm going to do to you, huh?"

"You'll just kill me, he'll kill me and my family." Rondo answered.

"Harlem, why don't you rock that girl's world for me please?"

"No problem boss." He answered as he pulled out his colt forty-five and pulled the trigger.

"Boom." The forty-five thundered as he shot Wendy in the back of her throat spraying her blood all over Rondo's face.

Rahman was laying in the woods and saw when Vinny and his men entered the mansion, but was not alarmed by their presence seeing that they were from some electrical company. Seeing the three guys in the black Suburban get out strapped with AR-15's caused his senses to go up. Still he waited and remained still. Rondo had twenty-four hours. A few minutes later he heard a loud sound, it was a single gunshot. Rahman pulled out his phone and call King Charles.

'Ring' 'Ring'.

"Son." King Charles answered.

"I think we have a problem papa."

"I'm listening."

"Justice has taken over the mansion, what do you want me to do?"

"Shit, damn Santiago's kill them take as many out as you can and get back home A.S.A.P."

"Yes sir, I'll take care of it." Rahman said before hanging up.

After returning the phone back to the pocket in his book bag he looked through the scope of his camouflaged sniper rifle and spotted one of the men dressed in a company uniform holding a pistol in his hand. He steady his breathing then took the shot. 'Bang.' The guy dropped like a sack of potatoes, after seeing his kill he broke down his rifle and strapped it to his book bag and slung it around his shoulders then pulled out his twin Glocks and headed to the mansion.

"Now that you see I'm not here to play tell me where can I find King Charles." Justice demanded.

"You tell him what he wants to know or die." Amir said as he pulled out his Glock and pointed it at Rondo's head.

"All I know is that he's in Atlanta I don't know exactly where." Rondo answered.

"I'm sorry to hear that."

"Why."

"Now you're no use to me, Amir kill him." Justice ordered.

Amir pulled the trigger blowing Rondo's brains all over the floor.

"That's for Red Bull." Amir whispered to himself as he tucked his gun away.

"Let's get outta here." Justice said then all five of them walked downstairs all of a sudden shots rang out and Justice found himself on the floor with Vinny on top of him there was blood all over his body but it wasn't his it was Vinny's.

"Stay down." Harlem World screamed. "He's in the house."

'Bang' 'Bang' 'Bang'. Amir began to shoot back Justice pushed Vinny's dead body to the side and got to his feet pulling his .357 he looked around still confused then he spotted Vinny's soldier dead on the floor not too far from Vinny.

"Get the fuck down Justice." Harlem World screamed again

seeing the assassin he ran towards Justice firing his Glock. 'Bloc' 'Bloc'. The assassin dropped for cover Justice and Harlem World ran into the kitchen for cover.

"Yo, who the fuck is this guy." Harlem World asked.

"I don't know, but whoever he is he's good."

'Bloc' 'Bloc'.

"We gotta get outta here we're sitting ducks." Justice said as he stood up and sprinted out the kitchen door firing his .357. 'Boom' 'Boom'. Blasting two holes in the wall barely missing the assassins head. Justice and Harlem World gave chase when they got to the living room they both froze. The assassin had Amir at gun point.

"This is where it ends Justice, both of your drop your fucking weapons." Rahman ordered.

"Who the fuck are you?" Justice asked.

"I'm the Devil himself now drop your fucking weapons or your friend dies."

Justice and Harlem World lowered their guns and let them fall to the ground.

"King Charles sends his regards." Rahman said pulling the trigger hitting Justice in his chest and stomach.

Before Rahman could get off a third shot Harlem World drew his .38 from the small of his back and dumped three rounds in the assassin's chest knocking him out the window. Amir reached down on the floor and picked up his Glock and ran to the window thinking he would see the assassin, but he was gone. Turning back to check on his friend he saw Harlem World holding Justice in his arms, he was unconscious, but he was still breathing.

"We gotta get him to the hospital. Pick him up and take him to the truck." Amir ordered. Harlem World complied picking Justice up. He single handedly carried Justice to the truck and laid him inside the backseat. Amir hopped in the driver side and crunk the truck up.

"Come on, bruh! We don't have much time." Amir hollered.

Harlem World jumped in the passenger seat and Amir sped

off headed to Charlotte Medical Center.

"Hold on Jus we're almost there man hold on." Harlem World screamed. "Don't slow down run the lights."

Within minutes they were pulling up at the hospital Amir pulled right up to the front door of the emergency room. Harlem World jumped out and opened the back door and grabbed Justice while Amir ran inside to get help. In seconds doctors were rushing out with stretchers. Once they got him loaded they rushed Justice inside for emergency surgery. Amir and Harlem World wanted to stay with him but they couldn't it was too dangerous the police would come asking a thousand questions all of which they had no answers to. They did the only thing they could do which was to leave they hopped back in the truck and hit the interstate. On the way down the highway Amir had called Lisa.

'Ring' 'Ring' 'Ring'.

"Hello." Lisa answered.

"Lisa."

"Yeah, who is this?"

"It's Amir, Justice has been shot."

"What, oh my God, is he okay?"

"I don't know I think it's pretty serious. He's at Charlotte Medical Center. I need you to get in your car and go there now."

"You left him."

"We couldn't stay Lisa that's why I'm calling you."

"Damn you Amir, I'm on the way out the door now." Lisa replied.

'Click.'

"She hung up." Amir said looking at Harlem World.

"Is she on the way?"

"Yeah."

"That's all that matters, what do we do now."

"I'm heading back to Chapel Hill, so we can lay low until I hear back from Lisa."

"Cool, that sounds like a plan."

The next day Rahman walked into King Charles' mansion

with anger written all over his face. His brother Ra'mon was the first person that he saw.

"Where is dad at?" Rahman asked.

"He's in his treatment right now, you know how he is after that."

"I need to speak with him. I'm tired of all this senseless killing."

"Killing is what you were trained for brother."

"I know what the fuck I was trained for, but the old man is fucking crazy him and this stupid Santiago beef. He should have never interfered he should have let things play out."

"You know the old woman is coming now."

"What are you afraid?"

"No never, but I almost died yesterday those guys we are going up against are very good at what they do."

"And so are you."

"I am only one person."

"You were trained by the same master."

"Yes but I am the only one father sends. I do the dirty work while you sit in this prison with your feet kicked up pretending to guard the old man."

"You know he is sick, what are you saying that I am incapable." Ra'mon hollered as he stepped up in Rahman face. Knowing his brother Rahman braced himself for an attack.

"That is enough." King Charles hollered. "I will not have my sons fighting under my roof."

"I'm sorry father." Ra'mon pleaded.

"Silence, do not speak to me go and prepared the soldiers, Rahman is right Vidah will be visiting me soon."

Ra'mon did not say a word he just walked out of the room.

"Tell me Rahman, what happened?" King Charles asked.

"I did as I was told I killed three of them Justice was injured he took a hit to the chest and the stomach." Rahman explained.

"And Rondo?"

"He is dead Justice killed him."

"Did he talk, did he tell him our location?"

"I don't know I'm not sure."

"You're not sure?" King Charles hollered then he smacked Rahman across the face.

"Father."

"I told you to clean it up."

"I did the best I could and almost died in the process."

"I will hear no more I have to rest."

"Do you not care, what is wrong with you? This war is stupid the Santiago's will unite and wipe us out you should have stayed out of it father."

"I could not stand by and watch my grandson dishonored. I had to roll the dice. I would have did it for you son, I would have done the same for you."

Hearing that Rahman was defeated and at a loss for words instead of arguing farther he remained silent and helped his old man to his room so he could rest.

"I know she will come when she does promise me that you will do nothing. Your brother doesn't understand but you do you are smarter than him. Do not let him kill her this war will end with me. When I'm gone I want you and your brother to take care of Amanda. Everything you need is in my warehouse in Charlotte make sure you get the tapes. Promise me son."

"I promise." Rahman replied as he watched his old man lay back on the bed.

"I have put things in motion others will die before me. I will rest easy in the end." King Charles said then he drifted off to sleep.

Lisa made it to Charlotte Medical in record time, when she got there Justice had just gotten out of surgery and was in stable condition. He was still unconscious when she walked into his room, he was hooked to a breathing machine helping him breathe. The doctor informed her that the bullet that entered his chest had punctured his lung and he would have to stay on the machine until he healed and also had to have a bag hooked to his stomach so he could use the bathroom. He's lucky to be alive, Lisa thought to herself as she sat down next to him. Lisa rubbed Justice face. "I love you so much baby I need you to stay strong and pull through this for me and the lil life growing inside my stomach. We need you baby I'm sorry I didn't get a chance to tell you. I'm not going anywhere I'ma stay right here by your side. Amir and Harlem World are safe. I know if you were awake you would be concerned about them don't worry I'll be here when you wake up." Lisa whispered not knowing if he could even hear her or not. She wanted to call his grandmother Vidah but it was late so she laid back and drifted off to sleep with Justice's hand in hers. The next morning when she had awakened Justice was still heavily sedated and unconscious she stood up and kissed him on the forehead and then walked out of the room to the lobby where she pulled out her phone and called Vidah Santiago, Justice's grandmother.

'Ring' 'Ring' 'Ring'.

"Hello." Vidah answered.

"Mama Santiago this is Lisa."

"Hey baby, I was just thinking about you, how are doing?"

"I'm fine, I have some bad news." Lisa replied and then got a lil quiet.

"What is it baby spit it out."

"Justice was shot last night Mrs. Santiago."

"He was what?" Vidah paused to get herself together, thinking maybe she didn't hear Lisa correctly.

"Somebody shot him."

"Is he okay?"

"He is in stable condition, but he's unconscious I stayed with him last night."

"What hospital are ya'll in?"

"We're at Charlotte Medical Center."

"Okay, me and Zeenah are on the way now."

"We're in room 247."

"Everything will be okay Lisa, I'll see you in a couple hours."

"Zeenah wake up baby get dressed." Vidah said.

"Grandma I'm tired." Zeenah replied wiping the cold out of her eyes.

"I don't care, somethings happened to your brother, we gotta get to the hospital."

"What happened is he okay?"

"Girl, stop asking me questions and get dressed now." Vidah hollered.

Hearing her grandma holler Zeenah got up and got dressed knowing that her grandmother never raised her voice, so she knew then whatever was going on had to be serious. Vidah shot to her bedroom and packed a light bag continued with blankets and extra clothes then she sat on her bed and put her face in her hands. She cried to herself knowing that whatever happened to her grandson was her fault. She should have never brought him into this life. It was too late for regrets now. What's done is done. Arturo would demand that she make amends, but she knew that, even Arturo knew he didn't have to tell her that. Wiping her tears Vidah got up off the bed and walked to her closet and pulled out an old shoe box. After pulling it out she stared at it for a second before she opened it. Sitting back on the bed she opened the box it was an old Taurus nine millimeter equipped with two clips and a silencer. It was her husband Raymond's old gun she had held onto it for years waiting for this day to come.

"Grandma I'm ready." Zeenah hollered from the next room.

"Okay baby I'm coming." Vidah replied hearing her granddaughters voice had snapped her out of her thoughts then she pulled the old nine and the clips and the silencer out of the box and stuffed it into her pocketbook then sling the strap over her shoulders.

"Zeenah come in here and grab this bag so we can go."

Her granddaughter complied and came in and grabbed the bag and carried it to the car. Vidah followed right behind her with her keys and her pocketbook then they both got in the car headed to Charlotte. After a two and a half hour drive they finally arrived at Charlotte Medical Center. Vidah parked her car then they both went inside and took the elevator to room 247. When they got to the door Vidah took a deep breath not knowing what to expect she kissed her granddaughter on the forehead then they both walk inside. Vidah was immediately at a loss for words. She had never seen her grandson like this before. He had tubes and I.V's running through his body and was hooked to a ventilating machine to help him breathe. She took a few steps closer and Justice looked like he was sleeping. She didn't notice Lisa as she walked up and gave Zeenah a hug because she was crying.

"Hey Lisa." Vidah greeted.

"Hey mama Santiago."

"Are you okay?"

"Yes."

"Good." Vidah replied then she sat beside her grandson and rubbed his hand.

"Everything will be okay baby grandma will take care of this, so don't worry, you just get better."

Vidah then stood up and pulled two blankets out of her bag she handed one to Zeenah and the other to Lisa. "These will keep you both warm. I don't want either of you to leave this room until I get back."

"Grandma where are you going?"

"I have something I have to take care of for your brother. I don't have time to explain."

"When are you coming back?"

"I'll be back in the morning in time for breakfast." Vidah answered as she gave Zeenah a hug then she turned and looked at Lisa and walked over and gave her a hug. "You stay strong for my grandson you hear me, he loves you very much."

"I will mama Santiago, you be careful, you're not as young as you used to be."

"I see Justice has been talking to you. Age ain't nothing but a number baby. I'm still the Queen." Vidah replied then smiled at Lisa as she walked out the door.

Getting in her car Vidah turned on some Marvin Gaye then pulled out of the parking deck headed to Atlanta to see King Charles.

After another painful three-hour drive to Atlanta, Vidah was finally pulling up at King Charles' mansion. At the gate house she rolled the window down in her 745 BMW to speak with the guards.

"Ma'am you cannot come inside at this time." The guard said.

"I'm here to see King Charles tell him Vidah Santiago is here."

"Ma'am it's 9pm he may be sleeping."

"Then I suggest you wake him up."

The intercom came on. "I am awake Victor let the woman thru." King Charles ordered.

"Yes sir." The guard said knowing King Charles was watching the cameras. He hit the button opening the gate. "I'm sorry ma'am you can enter now."

"It's okay." Vidah replied then drove her car thru the gate and to the front of the mansion. Checking her purse she pulled out Raymond's old Taurus 9mm and screwed the silencer on and popped the clip in and snatched the slide back allowing the hollow tip to enter the chamber then she returned the gun to her purse slung it over her shoulder and got out of her car. When she got to the front door she recognized the two huge men that were blocking the entrance.

"You were kids the last time I seen you two, do you know who I am?"

"Vidah Santiago." Rahman answered then he noticed Ra'mon slowly reach for his gun. "No brother that is not wise."

"Listen to your brother Ra'mon. I have no beef with you I am only here to see Charles."

"Let her in Ra'mon." King Charles hollered from the top of the stairs.

Hearing the old man's voice Ra'mon and Rahman both stepped aside and let Vidah walk into the mansion.

"Come to my office Vidah, we have much to discuss."

Vidah slowly walked up the stairs no longer paying the two brothers any mind. She followed Charles to his office and watched as he slowly sat behind his desk.

"Have a seat Vidah it's been a long time."

Vidah loosened up a lil bit and walked over to Charles and gave him a hug before she sat down on the other side of his desk.

"How are you doing Charles, you do not look so good these days."

"As you know I am very sick I am dying slowly but my boys they don't understand."

"I know Justice is the same way they think that we are supposed to live forever." Vidah chuckled. "I spared you years ago Charles, why did you interfere you knew the rules?"

"Your grandson dishonored Mikal by throwing his body out on the streets like some stray dog. I could not let that go unanswered."

"Instead you chose to bring death to your front door."

"I rolled the dice and I lost Vidah. I am dying anyway. I do not fear death."

"What about Amanda I know she still lives."

"That is why I let you walk right in here I want this war to end with me. All I ask is that you spare my granddaughter and my boys. They are too young to understand who they are up against."

"I cannot make you a promise on what you ask, if Justice dies everyone you've ever known will die in return and that I will personally oversee myself." Vidah answered as she dug in her purse and removed the Taurus 9mm that was hidden inside. "You see this gun here." Vidah held it up. "This gun belonged to my husband it was one of his favorites. I held on to it because I knew this moment would come and I would have my chance to avenge him."

"Raymond was my friend Vidah." King Charles replied as he grabbed his cigar and lit it up. "But he couldn't have expect me to kill my brother Hector, not even for him Vidah. Family is everything."

"Do not speak my husband's name." Vidah replied then kissed the barrel of her silencer. *I have avenged you Raymond, now you can rest easy.* Vidah thought to herself, then pointed the gun at King Charles face. "You were right Charles family is everything."

"See you in hell Vidah." King Charles replied right before Vidah pulled the trigger splattering his brains all over the wall. Vidah sighed and placed the old gun back inside her purse then she got up and walked out of King Charles' office. Not even taking a second look at his dead body. When she got to the bottom of the stairs Ra'mon drew his pistol and pointed it at her face. "I should fucking kill you." Ra'mon spat.

"Go ahead I'm a old woman I have lived my life but if you do this everyone you know will die."

"Ra'mon nooo. What are you doing?" Rahman hollered drawing his own pistol and pointing it at his brother.

"You would kill your own brother for this woman. She killed our old man Rahman."

"I can't let you kill her Ra'mon. The war is over now. It died with the old man. Don't you see we have to stop this?"

"That's where you're wrong brother." Ra'mon said tightening his grip. Rahman knew his brother like the back of his hand. He also tightened his grip on his Glock 40 and took the shot 'Bloc'. Hitting his brother in the shoulder causing him to drop his gun on the ground. Vidah looked down at a bleeding Ra'mon and smiled at him, then she looked at Rahman and her smile disappeared. "Because of Charles you both will get a pass. If I ever see ya'll again you both will die." Vidah spat then continued her stride walking past Rahman and the group of soldiers parted like the Red Sea and allowed the old woman to get back in her car and drive away. *Damn that is a powerful woman* Rahman thought to himself.

3 days later Butner Federal Correctional

Christopher Perry, Justice's father was on the yard lifting weights when he heard his name called over the intercom to report to receiving. He was a bit confused but thought maybe it was a piss test or something of that nature. When he walked in receiving he was surprised to see a Federal Marshall Officer with a set of full restraints in his hand.

"Christopher Perry."

"Yes."

"Let me see your I.D."

Chris handed it over. "What am I down here for?" Chris asked.

"You're shipping."

"What, I don't have a transfer in."

"Don't need one you know how the feds work you've been in the system long enough." The Marshall said as he handed Chris back his I.D.

"I need to put these restraints on you so I can get you to the airport." The Marshal said then began cuffing Chris and placing his restraints on. After the Marshal checked and double checked Chris he led him out to his transport vehicle then drove him to the RDU where he boarded a plane headed to San Diego Federal Penitentiary also known as the High Rise. After about four and a half hour flight the plane finally landed. Christopher was then transported to one of the roughest prisons in the federal system. When he entered receiving the Marshal that had transported him removed his restraints and wished him good luck before he left. Christopher was then taken to a private room where he was strip searched and given a different set of clothes.

"Welcome to Skyline Maximum Security Prison, are you affiliated with anything?" The federal correctional asked as he checked his property.

"No I'm not in a gang."

"Okay you're clean, here's your unit and cell card."

Chris took the cards and grabbed his property then headed to his housing unit. When he got inside he was surprised to see that he was surrounded by Mexicans. Paying it no mind, he went to his assigned cell and put his property down and began unpacking. The first thing he did was place his pictures on his locker as he looked at them he stopped on an old picture of himself, his wife Danielle and his baby son Justice. The good times of his past came flashing back then his thoughts were interrupted as four Mexicans with cartels tattoos walked into his cell.

"What's up?" Chris asked clearly unafraid.

"Your name Chris?" One of the Mexicans asked.

"Yeah that's me, what you still standing there for?"

The Mexicans were taken aback by his bluntness then two of them pulled out shanks. Chris squared his feet and his shoulders ready for the attack that was to come. "This is for the King." One of the Mexicans said then he attacked swinging his shank. Chris ducked the first swing and punched the Mexican in the ribs then he hit him with a right cross dropping the Mexican and knocking him out cold. The second Mexican attacked stabbing him in the shoulder. Chris hit him with a thundering uppercut under his jaw that knocked him back into the other two Mexicans. Seeing that they were off guard he rushed them trying to get himself out of the cell so he could have more room to fight. His plan didn't work. The other two Mexicans had moved out the way and then closed on him and stabbed him twice in the back blood was everywhere, but still Chris stood on his feet and faced the other three Mexicans another lunged at him he caught the Mexicans wrist and twisted his arm down stabbing the Mexican in the stomach with his own shank. He held the Mexican for a while before letting his body fall to the floor then he taunted the remaining two. "This is all you got, this is all the great King Charles can send. He didn't tell you I was built for this combat shit huh."

Chris hollered.

Just as Chris was about to attack the remaining two Mexicans someone grabbed him from behind in a choke hold then he felt the cold steel as it slid across his neck. Chris tried to grab his attacker but he couldn't move. The last thing he saw was the other two Mexicans stab him in the stomach then there was nothing but darkness his last thoughts were of his son, Justice.

A week later Justice had awakened from his induced coma. Seeing his family all together supporting him brought tears to his eyes. He looked around there were balloons and flowers everywhere. His grandmother and Lisa were holding his hand and his sister Zeenah was curled up in a blanket laying on the couch. Lisa was the first to notice that he had opened his eyes because she had felt him squeeze her hand.

"My baby's awake." Lisa hollered excited.

"Justice baby." Mama Santiago began to cry as she rubbed her grandson's arm.

"Zeenah wake up your brother's awake." Lisa said shaking Zeenah.

"Huh oh my God Justice." Zeenah said as she shot from under her blanket rushing to her brother's side.

"I'm so proud of you baby. I prayed for you. I knew your work wasn't finished here. How you do feel?"

"Thank you grandma." Justice said trying to move.

"Not too fast slow down."

"Chuckling. I'm still a lil sore. I'll heal soon. I have to finish what I've started grandma."

"No you don't all you have to do is get well." Vidah replied then she leaned over and whispered in Justices ear. "It's already finished you don't have to worry about Charles I've taken care of him." Vidah informed then stood up and winked her eye. "Someone's outside to see you." Vidah smiled. "Amir come in here.

Justice is awake."

Hearing the good news Amir walked inside the hospital room. "Damn boy I'm glad you're awake now I can get me some sleep." Amir chuckled.

"Shut up fool." Justice laughed.

"I'm serious your grandma is very demanding. She called and made me and Harlem come back up here and guard you."

"Where's Harlem, he saved my life?"

"He's outside watching the parking lot you already know how paranoid he is."

"Yeah I know. I tell you what I gotta get outta this hospital."

"It's already been arranged Justice. All we've been waiting for is for you to wake up."

Epilogue

After a short ride from Charlotte medical, they were finally landing on the Burlington's mansion helipad. Justice slowly stepped of the helicopter. He was accompanied by his grandmother, and his sister, and loyal general Amir. slowly they all walked inside, where Lisa and Harlem were waiting with the doctor.

"Hey baby," Lisa greeted as she walked over and gently hugged her man.

"Lisa damn its good to see you. I missed you," Justice uttered

"I know you! I missed you too. You're home now . I personally picked out a doctor to help you get better. He's upstairs making the room comfortable". Lisa informed.

"I know he's not in our bedroom," Justice replied a lil frustrated.

"Baby stop it you just got home. Don't you start." Lisa uttered, then went on and greeted the rest of the family.

"Come on let's go upstairs," Lisa said to Justice after she hugged Vidah.

Helping him to their room was a slow process, mainly because Justice now had to walk with a cane. When they reached the bedroom, the doctor was sitting on their bed. Seeing the couple walk in, the doctor stood and introduced himself.

"Hi! I'm Dr Street. I'll be overseeing your rehabilitation process." Dr Street said sticking his hand out.

Justice looked at the doctor's hand for a brief second before shaking it and introducing himself also.

"I'm Justice, nice to meet you. I know you're here to help; but I'll appreciate it if you don't make yourself at home in my bedroom." Justice said.

"Oh I'm sorry. I didn't mean to offend you. I was just trying to make the room comfortable for you." Dr Street replied.

"No offense taken. You didn't have to apologize. I just wanted us to have a understanding."

"Trust me I understand completely," Dr Street replied

"Justice, stop giving the doctor a hard time. He's just here to help you." Lisa spat getting a lil upset.

Sensing the frustration in his woman's voice, Justice decided to pipe down since this was his first time meeting the doctor. She was right, he was just there to help.

"Sorry bae," Justice said.

"I bet," Lisa shot back.

"Really baby I am." Justice replied as he walked up to her and pulled her to him by the small of her back. She was so close that he could feel the warmness of her breath. Lisa gasped in surprise.

"Well this is my cue. Mr Santiago, Mrs O'Neal, I'll be leaving now. I'll be back tomorrow at four." Dr Street informed.

"That will be fine," Lisa answered.

"See you tomorrow doc. Hey huh I didn't mean to jump down your throat earlier," Justice said

"Not a problem. I understand how you feel." Dr Street replied, then headed out the door.

"I don't want you to run him away with your attitude. You need him right now," Lisa said.

"I'll try, you know I don't like strange people in our home. After all we've been through, we can only trust our people," Justice informed.

"I know that Justice;but I picked this man myself. He's really good at what he does. Trust me on this please," Lisa replied.

"I do trust you. He's still here right?" Justice questioned right before Amir walked into the room.

Lisa was glad to see him, because right now she wasn't getting through to justice. He was just to stubborn. "Baby ima let you talk to your friend, okay? I'm going downstairs. Push the call button if you need me," Lisa said.

"Alright," Justice replied lightly brushing his hand across her butt. When she turned around he saw the smile on her face and returned it, silently communicating with her while he watched her strut seductively out the door.

"Come on, snap out of it," Amir interrupted laughing at Justice

"Shut up. Don't be mad at me because you don't have a girl." Justice shot back jokingly.

"Ain't no shortage of pussy my way. I just don't have time. I've been to busy guarding you." Amir stated

"I feel you. I can't wait til I heal up. I can't be doing this bed rest shit and that's a big triple fact."

"Just take your time. Mrs Santiago and Mrs O'Neal can run things until you're fully healed. I'm glad you're home." Amir said

"I'm glad to be home."

"We have some unfinished business that needs to be taking care of." Amir said as he placed his hand on his friend's shoulder.

"Torres." Justice whispered.

"Yea you know we can't let what happened to Red Bull slide. He was like a brother to me. We even the score. It's the only way I'll be about to sleep at night," Amir replied.

About the Author

Durell Eubanks is a native from Burlington, North Carolina. His passion for writing stems from the many days and nights spent inside of a prison cell, having to use his imagination to escape his confinement. He is the Author of I am Tony Blanco and Cartel City, novels filled with plenty of street action. Many people ask, "how does he come up with this stuff?" He would simply say, "I live inside my head." Currently he resides inside of his prison cell where he continues to put his pen to work.

Coming Soon:

Cartel City 2
Kingdom of Wolves

DURELL EUBANKS

www.ingramcontent.com/pod-product-compliance
Lightning Source LLC
Chambersburg PA
CBHW071956070526
44583CB00015B/1215